What I can say

1

My workbook

This workbook belongs to: _____
Age: _____
School: _____
Class: _____
Home address: _____
Phone number: _____

1 Listen!

These three boys are all called David. Listen and say which David is speaking. Tick (✓) the right picture.
Diese drei Jungs heißen alle David. Höre zu und sage, welcher David spricht. Mache ein Häkchen unter das richtige Bild.

2 Hoover's 'Book of Friends'

Listen to the CD and complete the page from the Book of Friends for the dog.
Höre genau zu und vervollständige die Seite aus dem Book of Friends für den Hund.

Luna
Blacky

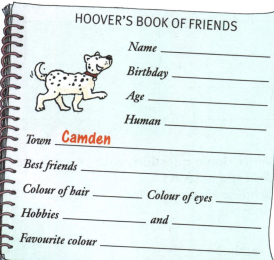

HOOVER'S BOOK OF FRIENDS
Name _____
Birthday _____
Age _____
Human _____
Town **Camden**
Best friends _____
Colour of hair _____ Colour of eyes _____
Hobbies _____ and _____
Favourite colour _____

3 Numbers

Write down the words for the numbers.
Schreibe die Zahlwörter im Kreuzworträtsel auf Englisch.

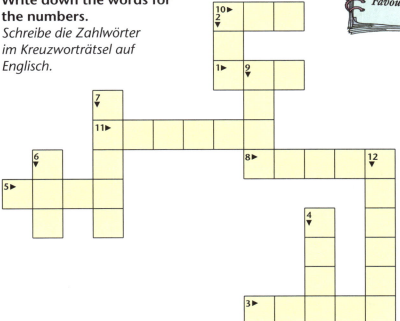

New friends

 4 **In the street**

a) Look at the picture. Name the people and things with words from the list.
Sieh dir das Bild an. Benenne die Sachen und Personen mit Wörtern aus der Liste.

a bag • a bike • a boy • a bus • a bus stop • a car • a cat • a dog • a flower
a girl • an ice cream • a lamp • an old man • a shop • a tree • a woman

1 _____ 5 _____ 9 _____ 13 _____

2 _____ 6 _____ 10 _____ 14 _____

3 _____ 7 _____ 11 _____ 15 _____

4 _____ 8 _____ 12 _____ 16 _____

b) Write down questions with *Where is the …?* about the things, people and animals in the picture. Add the answers.
Schreibe Fragen mit Where is the …? *über die Sachen, Personen und Tiere in dem Bild auf. Ergänze die Antworten.*

at the bus stop   near a bus   in a shop   on the street   with a boy

1 *Where is the old man?*   *He is at the bus stop.*

2 *Where is the girl?*   *She is* _____

3 *Where is the flower?*   *It is in the boy's hand.*

4 _____

5 _____

6 _____

c) Work with a partner. Ask three questions about the picture. Can he/she answer them correctly?
Arbeite mit einem Partner/einer Partnerin. Stelle drei Fragen zum Bild. Kann er/sie sie richtig beantworten?

1 New friends

5 At Camden Market

What can the reporter see at the market? Write sentences with *there is* or *there are*.
Was sieht der Reporter auf dem Markt? Schreibe Sätze mit there is *oder* there are.

"… This is Radio Junior Europe, live from Camden Town, London. I'm here at Camden Market. There …"

There are …

There is …

1 <u>There is a bag.</u>　　　　　　　　　5 _____

2 _____　　　　　　　6 _____

3 <u>There are</u> _____　7 <u>There are boots.</u>

4 _____　　　　　　　8 _____

6 New friends

a) Fit the puzzle pieces together. Find out who has got what.
Setze die Puzzleteile zusammen. Finde heraus, was wem gehört.

b) Ask questions with *What has … got?* and *Who has got …?*
Stelle Fragen mit What has … got? *und* Who has got …?

1 <u>What has Emma got?　　She has got a hamster.</u>

2 _____

3 _____

4 _____

5 <u>Who has got a camera?　　Caroline has.</u>

6 _____

7 _____

8 _____

New friends

7 Hi, I'm Spook.

a) **Listen and number the words from 1 to 8 in the order you hear them.**
Höre zu und nummeriere die Wörter von 1 bis 8 in der Reihenfolge, in der du sie hörst.

cats ☐   ice cream ☐   cold ☐   house ☐
funny ☐   sisters **1**   friend ☐   Polly ☐

Listen to Spook. Tick (✓) the right box.
Höre Spook genau zu. Hake das richtige Kästchen ab.

1 Spook is two ☐ three ☐ hundred years old.
2 Spook has got three brothers ☐ sisters ☐.
3 Spook lives in England ☐ Scotland ☐.
4 Spook's sisters have got three black ☐ blue ☐ cats.
5 Spook's two heads are for eating and sleeping ☐ playing and reading ☐.
6 Spook doesn't like steak and ice cream ☐ chicken and lemonade ☐.
7 Spook's best friend is a monster, Lizzie ☐ Nessie ☐.
8 Spook's best friend lives in Loch Ness ☐ Loch Tess ☐.

b) Now you. Choose words and write about yourself.
Jetzt du. Wähle Wörter aus und schreibe über dich.

I like _____, but I don't like _____.
I drink _____, but I don't drink _____.
I sing _____, but I don't sing _____.
I love _____, but I don't love _____.

dogs   goldfish   hip-hop
ice cream   cats   chicken
milk   pop songs   steak
water   rap   hamsters
cola   lemonade   words
rock songs   …

8 Say it in English

Was kannst du auf Englisch sagen, um …

1 … jemanden zu begrüßen?
   _____

2 … dich vorzustellen?
   _____

3 … jemand anders vorzustellen?
   _____

4 … jemanden nach seinem Namen zu fragen?
   _____

5 … jemanden zu fragen, woher er/sie kommt?
   _____

Where are you from?
This is …
What's your name?
Hi! Hello!
I'm …/My name is …

New friends

1

9 A cake, an ...

a) **Add *a* or *an*.**
Ergänze mit a oder an.

_____ cake   _____ apple   _____ snack

_____ orange juice _____ new football   _____ English girl

_____ partner   _____ ice cream   _____ game

b) **What is the rule? Find more examples.**
Wie heißt die Regel? Finde weitere Beispiele.

_____

_____

10 Meeting people

a) **Fill in the words.** *Setze die Wörter ein.*   am • is • are

I – _____   he – _____   she – _____

you – _____   they – _____

b) **Fill in the right forms of *be*.** *Setze die richtigen Formen von be ein.*

Hi. My name _____ Charlie. _____ you Caroline?

Yes, I _____. Where _____ you from, Charlie?

I'_____ from Notting Hill. Where _____ you from?

I'_____ from Manchester. _____ Rajiv your friend?

Yes, he _____. _____ Emma your new friend?

Yes, she _____ and so _____ Rajiv. They _____ very nice.

LiF 5

LiF 7

New friends

1

11 I, you, we, ...

Complete the sentences with the missing words.
Vervollständige die Sätze mit den fehlenden Wörtern.

LiF 6

1 Gillian is English. _____ is from Camden.

2 What about you? Where are _____ from?

3 My name is Charlie. _____ am from Notting Hill.

we • you • I • she • they • she • it • they

4 There are seven markets in Camden. _____ are great!

5 Charlie and Rajiv are from London. _____ are David's friends.

6 Butterfly is Gillian's cat. _____ is beautiful.

7 Gillian's house is small but _____ has got a nice garden.

8 My friends and I are at Haverstock School. _____ are in class 7 C.

LiF 8

12 What? When? ...

Use *what? when? where?* or *who?* to ask about the underlined parts of the sentences.
Benutze what? when? where? *oder* who?, *um nach den unterstrichenen Satzteilen zu fragen.*

1 David and Hoover are <u>in the park</u>.

   Where are David and Hoover?

2 <u>Emma</u> is at the market.

   Who is at the market?

3 That boy is <u>Rajiv Khan</u>.

   _____

4 David's birthday is <u>on 15th April</u>.

   _____

5 Haverstock School is <u>in Camden</u>.

   _____

6 Caroline can sing <u>funny songs</u>.

   _____

New friends

13 Caroline's friends

a) Complete the text with the missing words.
Vervollständige den Text mit den fehlenden Wörtern.

he • my • you • I • she
his • its • her • it • your

My name is Caroline Perrakis. _____'m from Manchester. I've got a brother. _____ name is George. Emma is _____ new friend. _____ is from Camden. _____ brother Jack sings in a band. Charlie is from Camden, too. _____ likes football. He has got a goldfish. _____ is orange. _____ name is Wanda. What's _____ name? Where are _____ from?

YOU: _____ name is _____. _____ am from _____.

b) Fill in the gaps. *Ergänze die Lücken.*

I – **my**

_____ – your

it – _____

he – _____

_____ – her

14 Charlie, Gillian and a dog

Can you write the words below the right pictures?
Kannst du die Wörter unter die richtigen Bilder schreiben?

she • her • its hat • a boy • its • it
her bike • a girl • his • a dog • its ball
he • his jeans • her sunglasses • his boat

_____   _____   _____
_____   _____   _____
_____   _____   _____
_____   _____   _____

15 Acrostic

Write your own name puzzle. Fill in what you like 🙂 and what you don't like ☹.
Schreibe dein eigenes Namensgedicht. Trage ein, was du magst 🙂 und was du nicht magst ☹.

PORTFOLIO

My body

16 A bathroom puzzle

Can you translate these words? They are hidden in the puzzle.
Kannst du diese Wörter übersetzen? Sie sind im Rätsel versteckt.

Arm _____
Badezimmer _____
Zahn _____
Junge _____
Haare _____
putzen _____
Hand _____
Mund _____
Gesicht _____
Wasser _____
Mädchen _____
Kopf _____
Spiegel _____
Ohr _____
waschen _____
Finger _____
Zeh _____

F	I	N	G	E	R	T	C
R	W	A	S	H	B	O	Y
E	C	A	F	O	A	E	C
C	O	D	W	A	T	E	R
L	G	D	A	E	H	I	I
E	I	N	E	A	R	L	A
A	R	A	T	O	O	T	H
N	L	H	T	U	O	M	E
R	O	R	R	I	M	R	A

The nine letters left over spell an animal. *Die neun Buchstaben, die übrig bleiben, ergeben ein Tier.*

17 The colour monster

a) Use the colour key to colour in the monster.
Benutze die Farblegende, um das Monster auszumalen.

Colour key
1 = brown
2 = black
3 = yellow
4 = green
5 = red
6 = blue

 b) Describe the monster's body.
Beschreibe den Körper des Monsters.

His head is …
His arms are …
His nose and ears are …
…

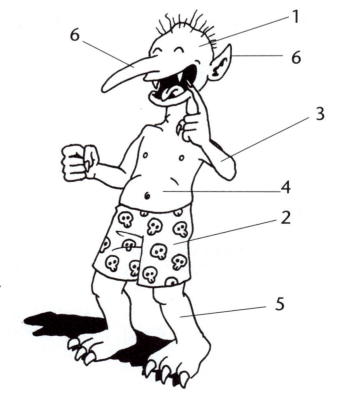

My body

1

18 Sounds

Say these words. Then make two lists.
Sprich die Wörter aus. Schreibe sie dann in die richtige Liste.

pet • friend • red
feet • clean • ~~we~~ • ~~yes~~
be • wet • teeth

[iː]	[e]
we	yes
_____	_____
_____	_____
_____	_____
_____	_____

WORDBANK B
The body

19 Parts of the body

Find the words for parts of the body and write them in the right place.
Finde die Wörter für die Körperteile und schreibe sie an die richtige Stelle.

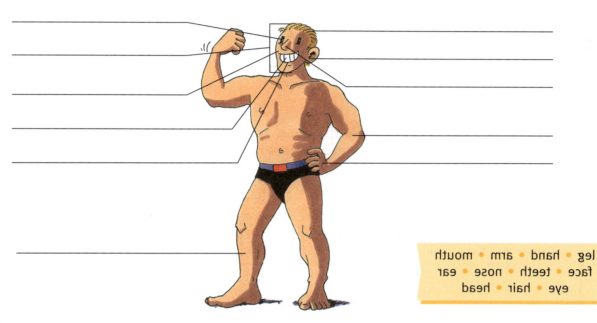

leg • hand • arm • mouth
face • teeth • nose • ear
eye • hair • head

TIP
Mit einem Spiegel kannst du die Lösungswörter sehen.

LiF 3

20 One or more?

Can you sort these words correctly with the sorting machine?
Kannst du diese Wörter mit der Sortiermaschine richtig verteilen?

friends   feet   bathroom   body   ear
rabbits   head   mouth   teeth   apples   face
table   shops   colour   clothes   schoolbag
boys   classrooms   legs   classmate

Einzahl (singular)   **Mehrzahl (plural)**

Unterstreiche die Wörter mit der Endung -s blau, alle anderen orange.

My body

21 Come on!

What's wrong here? Make correct sentences. *Was stimmt hier nicht? Bilde sinnvolle Sätze.*

LiF 12

hair • friend • milk • hands • song

Wash your books, please.

Ask your bus.

Sing a book.

Comb your teeth.

Drink your cake.

_____
_____
_____
_____
_____

22 Who am I?

a) Read the text and draw me in your exercise book. The red letters will help you to find my name! *Lies dir den Text durch und zeichne mich in deinem Heft. Die roten Buchstaben helfen dir, meinen Namen zu finden!*

Hi, everybody. I am a very funny monster. I live in Loch Ness in Scotland. I'm long and green. I have got a big body, a long neck and a small head. I have got two eyes like a fish. I have got four legs, two at one end of my body and two at the other end. I have got a long tail. I am a bit like a dinosaur and so I am very old. My best friends are Spook and his three sisters. I am very good at swimming. Oh, and I am a 'she'!

My name is _____.

b) Are the sentences true or false? Put a tick (✓) in the right box. *Sind die Sätze richtig oder falsch? Mache Häkchen in das richtige Kästchen.*

		true	false			true	false
1	The monster lives in Loch Ness.	☐	☐	4	The monster has got two eyes.	☐	☐
2	The monster is long and brown.	☐	☐	5	She has got two legs at the end of her body.	☐	☐
3	She has got a big body and a short neck.	☐	☐	6	She has got a long tail like a dinosaur.	☐	☐

c) Can you correct the wrong sentences? *Kannst du die falschen Sätze berichtigen?*

_____
_____

23 Opposites

Find the opposites. Draw lines.
Finde die Gegensätze. Ziehe Linien.

right   big   new   small   good   clean   tall
bad   white
        short   old   wrong
black   ugly   dirty   good-looking

24 Hobbies

a) Write the words in the correct list. *Schreibe die Wörter in die passende Liste.*

swimming, books, dog, football, skateboarding, rabbit, fish, coins, doll, music, cat, guitar, hockey, basketball, cage

hobbies	sport	pets
___	___	___
___	___	___
___	___	___
___	___	___
___	___	___

b) Match the words. Draw lines. *Finde die passenden Wörter. Ziehe Linien.*

play • collect • listen to • write • go • play • read • play • clean • meet

model cars • football • emails • swimming • friends • CDs • comics • the hamster cage • the guitar • games

WORDBANK C
hobbies and free time

25 Emma and Caroline

The sentence parts are in the wrong order.
Fill in the table correctly.
Die Satzteile sind in der falschen Reihenfolge. Trage sie richtig in die Tabelle ein.

1 Emma's room – loves – Caroline
2 are – Emma's DVDs – in a box
3 Emma – lots of DVDs – has got
4 is – Emma's hobby – animal films
5 cowboy films – can't stand – Caroline
6 till Monday – can have – the DVD – Caroline

	Subjekt (subject)	Verb (verb)	Objekt (object)	Ergänzung (other parts)
1	Caroline	loves	Emma's room.	
2	Emma's DVDs	are		in a box.
3				
4				
5				
6				

LiF 21

Hobbies

26 Ready, steady, GO!

You have got five minutes to write down all the hobbies you can think of.
Du hast fünf Minuten Zeit, um alle Hobbys aufzuschreiben, die dir einfallen.

_____

_____

_____

TIP
Bittet eure Lehrerin/ euren Lehrer, die Zeit zu stoppen.

27 John, Mike and Emma

a) **Look at the picture of John in his room. Then complete the text.**
Sieh dir das Bild von John an. Dann vervollständige den Text.

games • homework
sport • computer
posters • favourite

John's hobby is his _____. He has got five

_____. His _____ game is 'Masternet'.

He can do his _____ on the computer, too.

Football is his favourite _____. He has got a lot of

football _____.

b) **Look at Mike's notes about his hobby. Write a short text about his hobby.**
Sieh dir Mikes Stichwörter zu seinem Hobby an. Schreibe einen kurzen Text über sein Hobby.

Mike, 11
hobby: basketball
100 basketball cards
in basketball team
club: Camden Rabbits
club colours: green, yellow
can play in park
basketball games on TV

<u>Mike is eleven. His hobby is</u> _____

_____

_____

_____

 Look at the picture and write a text about Emma's hobby.
Sieh dir das Bild an und schreibe einen Text über Emmas Hobby.

_____

_____

_____

_____

_____

_____

Test yourself

Auf den *Test yourself*-Seiten hast du Gelegenheit zu überprüfen, was du in *Theme* 1 gelernt hast. Bearbeite erst einmal der Reihe nach alle Aufgaben und vergleiche deine Ergebnisse dann mit einem Partner oder einer Partnerin.
Überlege anschließend, welche Aufgaben dir leicht gefallen sind ☺, welche nicht ganz einfach waren 😐 und welche du richtig schwierig fandest ☹.
Die *Test yourself*-Seiten helfen dir bei deiner Selbsteinschätzung mit den Portfolio-Fragebögen.

1 Listening: New friends

Listen to the dialogue. Tick (✓) what you hear. *Höre dir den Dialog an. Hake ab, was du hörst.*

1 What's her ☐ your ☐ name?
2 I'm ☐ She's ☐ from Manchester.
3 Welcome to Manchester ☐ Camden ☐.
4 I've got a collection of comics ☐ CDs ☐.
5 His ☐ Her ☐ name is Butterfly.
6 I love ice cream ☐ cats ☐.

2 Speaking: Can you say it in English?

Match the sentences. *Verbinde die passenden Sätze.*

Was sagst du, wenn du fragen willst,

1 … ob jemand ein Haustier hat?
2 … wie jemand heißt?
3 … wie es jemandem geht?
4 … wo jemand herkommt?
5 … wie die Telefonnummer von jemandem lautet?
6 … ob jemand eine Postkartensammlung hat?

R What's your name?
E Where are you from?
D Have you got a collection of postcards?
F Have you got a pet?
N What is your telephone number?
I How are you?

1	2	3	4	5	6

3 Words: Odd one out

Which word is the odd one out? *Welches Wort passt nicht zu den anderen?*

1 boy – girl – brother – sister – dog   _____
2 red – leg – knee – head – arm   _____
3 fish – nice – duck – dog – cat   _____
4 brown – red – dirty – blue – black   _____
5 milk – water – game – orange juice – tea   _____
6 skirt – trousers – shoe – camera – T-shirt _____

Friends

4 Reading: Charlie Batson

Read about Charlie Batson. Tick (✓) if the sentences are true or false.
Lies den Text über Charlie Batson. Entscheide, ob die Sätze wahr oder falsch sind, und mache Häkchen.

> Hello. I'm Charlie Batson. I'm twelve and I live in Camden. I've got two sisters. Sharon is seven and Josephene is eighteen. My best friends are David Williams and his dog, Hoover, and Emma Butler. We are in class 7C at Haverstock School. I like football and I'm in the junior football team at school. My favourite football club is Arsenal. I have got a goldfish and I'm president of the school goldfish club.

	True	False	Not in the text
1 Charlie is twelve years old.	☐	☐	☐
2 He lives in Camden.	☐	☐	☐
3 Charlie lives in School Road.	☐	☐	☐
4 His best friends are David, Hoover and Josephine.	☐	☐	☐
5 He is in class 7B at Haverstock School.	☐	☐	☐
6 Charlie likes football.	☐	☐	☐
7 Charlie's goldfish is a 'she'.	☐	☐	☐
8 His favourite football club is Chelsea.	☐	☐	☐

5 Writing: An email

Write an email to a new friend. Ask two questions at the end. *Schreibe eine E-Mail an einen neuen Brieffreund bzw. an eine neue Brieffreundin. Stelle zum Schluss zwei Fragen.*

Hi, _____

My name is _____ and I live

_____. I go _____

_____ School. I'm _____ class _____ there.

My hair _____ and my eyes _____ .

My favourite colour _____ , my favourite animal _____

and my favourite sport _____ .

Are you _____?

What _____?

Goodbye

_____

1 New at school

a) Listen to the CD. How many different people can you hear? Tick (✓) the right box.
Höre dir die CD an. Sage, wie viele verschiedene Leute sprechen. Hake das richtige Kästchen ab.

I can hear   4 ☐   5 ☐   6 ☐   7 ☐   people.

b) Listen again. Link the people with the things. Who is left over?
Höre dir die CD nochmals an. Verbinde die Leute mit den Sachen. Wer bleibt übrig?

football   chair   guitar   goal

_____ is left over.

2 In your schoolbag

a) What have you got in your schoolbag? Put the letters in the right order.
Was ist in deiner Schultasche? Setze die Buchstaben in die richtige Reihenfolge.

1 _____
2 _____
3 _____
4 _____
5 _____
6 _____
7 _____
8 _____
9 _____
10 _____

1. clis**p**en
2. sne**p**
3. ko**b**os
4. **w**homroke
5. be**r**rub
6. **r**urel
7. ceasil**p**enc
8. el**u**g
9. **c**ultrocala
10. os**s**criss

b) Work with a partner. Ask six questions with *What is ... in English?*
Arbeite mit einem Partner. Stelle sechs Fragen mit What is ... in English?

You: What is *Hausaufgabe* in English?
Your partner: It's 'homework'. What is *Schultasche* in English?
You: It's 'schoolbag'. What is *Taschenrechner* in English?
Your partner: It's 'calculator'. What is ...?

What I can say 2

TIP Es hilft, wenn du auf die Anzahl der Namen achtest.

CD

WORDBANK D
school

In the classroom

3 Puzzle

What are the German words in English? What is the solution?
Wie heißen die Wörter auf Englisch? Wie lautet das Lösungswort?

Schrank	1
Kreide	2
Karte	3
Uhr	4
Schreibtisch	5
Mülleimer	6
Fenster	7
Stuhl	8
Boden	9
Tür	10

The solution is:
_____

LiF 2

4 How many?

Look at the picture on page 28–29 in your textbook again. Count the people, animals and things in the list and write out the numbers. Make sentences with *there is* or *there are*.
Sieh dir das Bild auf Seite 28–29 in deinem Buch noch mal an. Zähle die Personen, Tiere und Sachen in der Liste und schreibe die Zahlen in Worten auf. Bilde Sätze mit there is *oder* there are.

There is/are …

_____ boys   _____ mice
_____ chairs   _____ rulers
_____ computers   _____ sandwich
_____ desks   _____ schoolbags
_____ girls   _____ teacher

… in the classroom.

CD

5 Sounds

Höre dir die folgenden Wörter an.
Achte genau auf die Endungen, die du hörst. Ist es [s], wie in *say* oder [z], wie in *has*?
Versuche, nach dem zweiten Hören die Wörter zu schreiben. Dann lies sie deiner Nachbarin/deinem Nachbarn vor.

[s]   [z]
_____ _____   _____ _____

_____ _____   _____ _____

TIP
Sprich die Wörter mehrmals deutlich aus.

In the classroom

6 Say it in English

What do you say in English if ... *Was sagst du auf Englisch, wenn ...*

1 ... du von jemandem sein/ihr Buch leihen möchtest?
2 ... du jemanden bittest, dir bei einer Übung zu helfen?
3 ... du jemanden nicht verstanden hast?
4 ... du von deinem Nachbarn einen Bleistift haben willst?
5 ... du jemanden fragen möchtest, ob du das Fenster öffnen kannst?
6 ... du jemandem deine Hausaufgaben geben willst?
7 ... du nicht weißt, was 'rubber' auf Deutsch heißt?
8 ... du jemanden fragen willst, womit er nicht klar kommt?

(b) Have you got a pencil?
(o) Can I open the window, please?
(n) Sorry? Can you say that again, please?
(r) What's the German word for 'rubber'?
(p) Can I have your book, please?
(a) Here you are. My homework is in my book.
(i) Can you help me with this exercise?
(d) What's your problem?

Write the letters in here to find the solution.
Schreibe die Buchstaben hier hinein, um das Lösungswort zu finden.

The poster is on the

1	2	3	4	5	6	7	8

7 Can they or can't they?

Look at the pictures and answer the questions. *Sieh dir die Bilder an und beantworte die Fragen.*

1 Can this boy sing?

No, he can't.

What about this boy?

Yes, he can.

2 Can this boy play tennis?

_____

What about this boy?

_____

3 Can this girl play streetball?

_____

What about this girl?

_____

4 Can this bike go fast?

_____

What about this bike?

_____

In the classroom

8 Where are they?

Look at the seating plan and complete the sentences with words from the box.
Sieh dir den Sitzplan an und vervollständige die Sätze mit Wörtern aus dem Kästchen.

LiF 13

next to • in • in front of
next to • behind
between

1 Charlie is _____ David.
2 Mandy is _____ Caroline and Mark.
3 Jeff and Emma are _____ Jason.
4 Mark is _____ Gillian.
5 Gillian and David are _____ Charlie.
6 The pupils are _____ Mrs Honey's classroom.

LiF 4, 10

9 Short answers

Ask questions and give short answers. Use information from the table.
Stelle Fragen und gib Kurzantworten. Benutze die Informationen aus der Tabelle.

	have/has got		am / is /are	
	pet	brother	from Manchester	At Haverstock school
Charlie & David	✓	✗	✗	✓
Caroline	✓	✓	✓	✓
Rajiv	✗	✗	✗	✓

1 Have Charlie and David got a brother?   No, they haven't.
2 Has Caroline _____   Yes, she _____
3 Are Charlie and David from Manchester?   No, they aren't.
4 Is Rajiv _____   No, he _____
5 _____   _____
6 _____   _____
7 _____   _____
8 _____   _____

10 What's the time?

a) **Draw the hands on the clocks.** *Zeichne die Zeiger in diesen Uhren ein.*

three fifteen
quarter past three

five forty-five
quarter to six

nine thirty
half past nine

nine ten
ten past nine

eleven thirty-five
twenty-five to twelve

twelve fifty-three
seven minutes to one

b) **Write down the times.** *Schreibe die Uhrzeiten auf.*

It is _____

_____

_____

_____

_____

11 At the bus stop

Listen to the boys. When is their bus?
Höre den Jungen genau zu. Wann fährt ihr Bus?

Their bus is at _____

CAMDEN TOWN
8　00　10　20 and every 5 minutes until _
9　00　05　10　15　20　25　30　36　42　48　54
10　00　06　12 and every 6 minutes until _
11　00　06　12　18　24　30　40　50
p.m.
12　00　10　20 and every 10 minutes until _
1
2
3　00　05　10 and every 5 minutes until …

A lesson

12 Rajiv's maths lesson

Look at B5 on page 33 in your textbook. Tick (✓) the right boxes.
Sieh dir B5 auf Seite 33 in deinem Buch an. Hake die richtigen Kästchen ab.

Please listen to me in class!

1. Where is Rajiv?
   a) at home ☐
   b) at the youth club ☐
   c) at school ☐

2. What day is it?
   a) Monday ☐
   b) Thursday ☐
   c) Friday ☐

3. What is his last lesson?
   a) art ☐
   b) maths ☐
   c) English ☐

4. What is Rajiv not interested in?
   a) numbers ☐
   b) music ☐
   c) school ☐

5. Who is Rajiv dreaming about?
   a) Caroline ☐
   b) Mr Graham ☐
   c) David ☐

6. Why is Mr Graham not happy?
   a) because his face goes red ☐
   b) because Rajiv dreams in class ☐
   c) because the pupils jump up ☐

13 What can we do?

LiF 1R

a) Fill in + and −.
Trage + und − ein.

speak English | sing | make a poster | write a letter | run fast | make a poem | ride a bike | ...

I
My father
My mother
My teacher
My best friend
My pet −

b) Write eight funny sentences with *can* and *can't*. *Schreibe acht lustige Sätze mit* can *und* can't.

1 *My pet can't speak English.*
2 _____
3 _____
4 _____
5 _____
6 _____
7 _____
8 _____

c) Ask your neighbours what they can do. *Frage deine Nachbarinnen und Nachbarn, was sie können.*

Can you …?   Yes, I can.   No, I can't.

14 Gillian's Saturday

Cross out the wrong form of the verbs.
Streiche die falsche Form der Verben durch.

1 Gillian ~~get~~ / gets up at about 9 o'clock.
2 First, she and her mother has / have a big breakfast.
3 Then Gillian and her mother go / goes shopping.
4 Gillian often clean / cleans her room on Saturdays.
5 She sometimes meet / meets her friends at the market.
6 In the evening, Gillian listen / listens to a CD.
7 After that she and her mother often watch / watches TV.
8 Gillian always go / goes to bed very late on Saturday.

15 Whose ...?

Complete the sentences. *Vervollständige die Sätze.*

1 Hoover is ___David's___ dog.
2 Mr Graham is _____ maths teacher.
3 _____ hobby is her collection of CDs.
4 Jack is _____ brother.
5 Claire is _____ friend in Manchester.
6 _____ favourite sport is football.

16 At school

Put the words in the right order. *Schreibe die Wörter in der richtigen Reihenfolge auf.*

1 by bus – Chelsea – goes – always – to school

   ___Chelsea always goes to school by bus.___

2 never – to school – Charlie – comes – late

   _____ .

3 Mrs Priest's English lessons – enjoys – Rajiv – usually

   _____ .

4 Hoover – David – often – to the park – takes

   _____ .

5 the friends – at the market – sometimes – meet

   _____ .

6 Hoover – with Blacky and Luna – plays – usually

   _____ .

A school day

17 Days and weeks

LiF 14

Read Emma's diary. Write about her week. *Lies Emmas Terminkalender. Schreibe über ihre Woche.*

Monday:	clean the hamster cage
Tuesday:	go shopping with mum
Wednesday:	visit her friend Lucy
Thursday:	tidy my room
Friday:	go swimming
Saturday:	wash Dad's car
Sunday:	make breakfast

Monday

On Mondays Emma always cleans the hamster cage.

Read Rajiv's diary for Tuesday and write sentences. *Lies Rajivs Terminkalender für Dienstag und schreibe Sätze.*

Tuesday	
7:00	get up
8:15	go to school
12:30	meet Murat for lunch
15:30	go to music club
17:30	do homework
19:00	have dinner
20:00	play computer games

Tuesday

Rajiv gets up at seven o'clock in the morning.

 Look at the pictures and write about Charlie's week. *Sieh dir die Bilder an und schreibe über Charlies Woche.*

Monday

Tuesday

Wednesday

Thursday

Friday

Saturday

Sunday

_____
_____
_____
_____
_____
_____

18 Speech bubbles

Complete the speech bubbles.
Vervollständige die Sprechblasen.

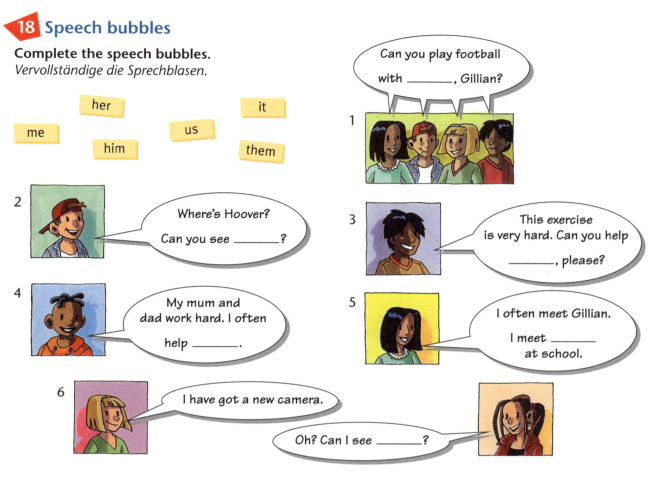

19 Alphabet

a) How long do you need to put these words in alphabetical order?
Wie lange brauchst du, um diese Wörter alphabetisch zu ordnen?

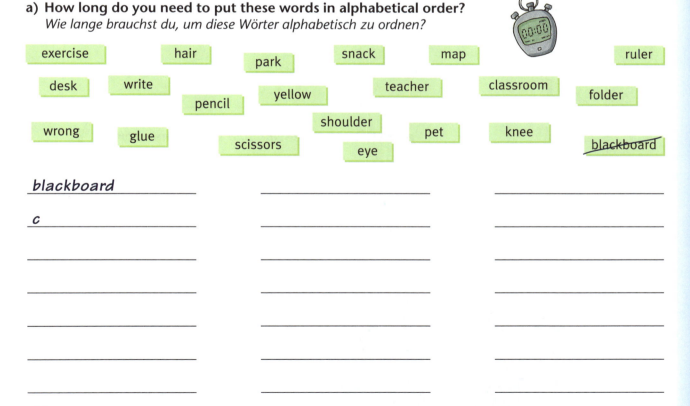

blackboard

c _____

b) Work with a partner. Spell a word and then check if it is right.
Arbeite mit einer Partnerin/einem Partner. Buchstabiere ein Wort und kontrolliere dann, ob es richtig geschrieben ist.

A school day

20 My timetable

WORDBANK D
school

a) Write down your timetable in English. *Schreibe deinen Stundenplan auf Englisch auf.*

Lesson	1	2	3	4	5	6
Monday						
Tuesday						
Wednesday						
Thursday						
Friday						

b) What are your favourite subjects? What subjects don't you like? Make lists.
Wie heißen deine Lieblingsfächer? Welche Fächer magst du nicht? Mache Listen.

I like:

1 _____
2 _____
3 _____

I don't like:

1 _____
2 _____
3 _____

c) Work with a partner. Talk and write about your lists.
Arbeite mit einer Partnerin/einem Partner. Rede und schreibe über die Listen.

My favourite subject is _____ and I like _____, too.

_____ is sometimes interesting and sometimes boring.

I don't like _____.

_____ is difficult for me.

21 Two schools

a) **Here are two jumbled texts about a school in Berlin and a school in London. Can you sort them out? Write G (= Germany) or GB (= Great Britain) in the boxes.**
Hier sind zwei Texte über eine Schule in Berlin und eine Schule in London durcheinander gemischt. Kannst du sie sortieren? Schreibe G bzw. GB in den Kästchen.

G	This is my school in Berlin.
	We get to school at about 7:50 and we go to our classroom.
	This is my school in London.
	The teacher comes at 8 o'clock and the first lesson starts.
	In Germany we stay in our classroom and the teachers come to us.
	We get to school at about 8:50 and we go to our form teacher's classroom.
	Our form teacher comes at 9 o'clock for registration. Then we go to our first lesson.
	Our lessons are 45 minutes, but there are some double lessons of 90 minutes.
	In Britain, the teachers stay in their classrooms and we go to them.
	We have got a 60-minute break between morning and afternoon lessons.
	Our lessons in London are 60 minutes, but there are no double lessons.
	At my school in Berlin, lessons finish at 1 o'clock.
	We stay after school for clubs.
	At my school, lessons finish at 3:30.

b) **What differences can you find? Make lists.** *Welche Unterschiede kannst du finden? Mache Listen.*

	Germany	Great Britain
go to school		
school starts		
lessons		
double lessons		
clubs		
school finishes		

c) **Write a text about your school in your exercise book.**
Schreibe einen Text über deine Schule in dein Heft.

Here are some ideas: where your school is • when school starts/finishes • how many lessons a day • what subjects you have • number of boys/girls in your class • what you like/don't like • …

A school day

22 ☼ Club cards

Choose a club and complete a club card.
Wähle einen Klub und fülle eine Klubkarte aus.

HAVERSTOCK SCHOOL FOOTBALL CLUB
Name: _____
Address: _____
_____
Age: _____

Have you got a) football boots?
b) a T-shirt and shorts?
c) time on Saturday afternoons?
Can you come to training on Wednesday evenings?

Yes ☐ No ☐
Yes ☐ No ☐
Yes ☐ No ☐
Yes ☐ No ☐

HSPC: Haverstock School Pet Club
Name: _____
Address: _____
_____
Age: _____
How many pets have you got? _____
What kind of pets have you got? _____
Do you want a pet? What kind? _____
Have you got time on Friday afternoons? Yes ☐ No ☐

23 What about you?

a) Write six sentences, three with *have to* and three with *don't have to*. Add your own ideas.
Schreibe sechs Sätze, drei mit have to und drei mit don't have to. Füge deine eigenen Ideen hinzu.

LiF 20

I have to clean my teeth.

	have to	clean my teeth. do my homework. go to school. help with the shopping. make my bed. play football. take the dog for a walk. watch TV. ...
I	don't have to	

I don't have to watch TV.

1 _____   4 _____

2 _____   5 _____

3 _____   6 _____

☼ **b) Write about yourself.** *Schreibe über dich.*

_____
_____
_____
_____

Test yourself

Die *Test yourself*-Seiten kennst du schon aus *Theme* 1. Bearbeite die Aufgaben nacheinander und vergleiche deine Ergebnisse dann mit einem Partner/einer Partnerin.
Überlege anschließend, welche Aufgaben dir leicht gefallen sind ☺, welche nicht so einfach für dich waren 😐 und welche du richtig schwierig fandest ☹. Fülle dann den Portfolio-Fragebogen für *Theme* 2 aus.

1 Listening: Emma and Jack

Listen to Emma and Jack, and tick (✓) if the statements are true or false.
Höre dir Emma und Jack an und hake ab, ob die Aussagen richtig oder falsch sind.

		true	false
1	The dialogue is about Emma's new timetable.	☐	☐
2	Jack doesn't like his timetable.	☐	☐
3	Monday is Emma's favourite day.	☐	☐
4	Emma has got French in the first two lessons.	☐	☐
5	After French, Emma has got two lessons of maths.	☐	☐
6	After lunch, Emma goes to Mrs Gregg for science.	☐	☐
7	Jack thinks that Mrs Gregg is nice.	☐	☐
8	Emma likes science, but she can't stand Mrs Gregg.	☐	☐

2 Reading: Camden Dog School

Read the text about Hoover's school. Then cross out the wrong words.
Lies den Text über Hoovers Schule. Dann streiche die falschen Wörter durch.

> Hoover goes to Camden Dog School every Saturday. School starts at half past nine and finishes at eleven o'clock. There is a break from ten o'clock to a quarter past ten. Hoover's best friend, David, goes to school, too. But David doesn't like the lessons – he likes the breaks. And Hoover? He loves the lessons, but the breaks are boring. When Hoover does an exercise right David says, "Oh, Hoover, you are the star! You are the champion!" Then Hoover gets a dog sweet. You can see why Hoover loves school!

1 Hoover goes to school / the park every Saturday.
2 School starts at half past nine / nine o'clock.
3 There is a break / lesson at 10 o'clock.
4 David doesn't like / likes the breaks at his school.
5 But Hoover finds the breaks at the dog school are boring / cool.
6 When Hoover does an exercise right / wrong, he gets a dog sweet.

3 Words: Time words

Can you complete these two lists? *Kannst du diese Listen vervollständigen?*

y	e	s	t	e	r	d	a	y
t								
t								

d	a	y	
w			
m			
y			

At school

2

4 Speaking: Say it in English, please.

Was kannst du auf Englisch sagen,

1 ... um jemanden zu fragen, wie spät es ist?
2 ... wenn du jemanden nicht verstanden hast?
3 ... wenn du von deinem Nachbarn einen Bleistift haben möchtest?
4 ... wenn du jemanden fragen möchtest, ob du das Fenster öffnen kannst?
5 ... wenn du nicht weißt, was 'bin' auf Deutsch heißt?

_____
_____
_____
_____
_____

von 10

5 Writing: Your favourite school day

**a) Which day is your favourite school day?
Fill in the timetable.**
*Was ist dein Lieblingsschultag?
Fülle den Stundenplan aus.*

lesson	Day
1	
2	
3	
4	
5	
6	

b) Write four sentences about your favourite school day this year.
Schreibe vier Sätze über deinen Lieblingsschultag in diesem Jahr.

1 My favourite day is _____ because I have _____
_____.

2 My first lesson _____ at _____ .

3 My second _____ . I like/don't like it because _____
_____.

4 My favourite lesson _____ at _____ . It _____ my
favourite because _____.

von 10

6 Grammar: Simple present

Which verbs take -(e)s? *Welche Verben benötigen -(e)s?*

1 Butterfly love [ ] fish.
2 Rajiv and Caroline dance [ ] at the party.
3 David get [ ] up early.
4 Gillian and her mother often go [ ] shopping.
5 Their break finish [ ] at 11 o'clock.

von 2,5

3 What I can say

1 Grandma Williams

a) Look at the picture and tick (✓) if the statements are true or false.

		true	false
1	The remote control is on the coffee table.	☐	✓
2	The keys are on the television.	☐	☐
3	The TV magazine is behind the cushion.	☐	☐
4	Grandma's glasses are on the sofa.	☐	☐
5	The teapot is on the big table.	☐	☐
6	The cups are on the coffee table.	☐	☐
7	Gillian is standing behind the sofa.	☐	☐
8	The flowers are on the big table.	☐	☐
9	The telephone is on the cupboard.	☐	☐
10	The shopping bag is next to the armchair.	☐	☐

b) Correct the four wrong statements.

Number 1 is wrong. The remote control is under the coffee table.

Number _____

_____

_____

2 YOUR room

a) Describe your room. Example: I've got two posters on my wall.

What have you got ...

1 ... on your wall? _____

2 ... next to your desk? _____

3 ... in your cupboard? _____

4 ... under your bed? _____

5 ... above your bed? _____

6 ... on your floor? _____

b) Make a picture dictionary for things in your room.

My room

3 Caroline's room

LiF 13

a) Look at page 48 in your textbook again. Complete the email with the words.

above • behind • between • in • in front of • next to • on • under • over • opposite

Hi Claire,

I love my new room because it's really big and it has got green walls. I've got a poster of my favourite band _____ the wall _____ my bed. I keep my books in a shelf _____ my bed. I've got an extra bed now. My friends can sleep there. Hope you can come in the next holidays ☺.

My desk is _____ the window. I usually do my homework there. It's nice because I can look out of the window if I need a break. My pinboard is _____ my desk. My desk is _____ my bed. My chest of drawers is _____ my wardrobe and the second bed. It's _____ from the window. My mum says I have to tidy my room. So I try to put all my clothes _____ my wardrobe, and the inline skates _____ my bed. It's hard, you know, my room is always a mess! But I usually make my bed every morning. How are you? Write back soon.

Love, Caroline xxx

b) What is it?

1. You can sleep there. _____
2. You can play your CDs in it. _____
3. You can put your clothes in it. _____
4. You can put your books on it. _____
5. You can do your homework at it. _____

4 A telephone call

a) Read the speech bubbles and number them.

No, George has got his own room. Don't worry.

Yes. Why?

OK. Call me later then. Bye.

Hi Emma! Do you want to come this afternoon and stay the night? I have an extra bed in my room. You can sleep there.

I can bring my new CD and we can dance and have fun. But I have to ask my mum first.

Have you got a CD player?

Oh, yes, that's a great idea. What about your brother? Does he sleep in your room too?

Sure. And Caroline, please don't tell George about my silly question. I think it's nice to have a girls' night only. Bye, now.

b) Listen to Caroline and Emma. Check the order of the speech bubbles.

5 A puzzle

Write the correct forms.

1 I play – he _plays_
2 he sits – my friends ___
3 we clean – you ___
4 you go – she ___
5 I feed – Charlie ___
6 they tidy – Gillian ___
7 you take – Sharon ___
8 we eat – it ___
9 my mother sleeps – I ___
10 they help – I ___
11 he does – they ___
12 he puts – she ___
13 I make – he ___
14 they like – I ___
15 we forget – Caroline ___
16 we keep – my parents ___
17 we watch – she ___
18 she asks – you ___

Now find your answers in this puzzle.

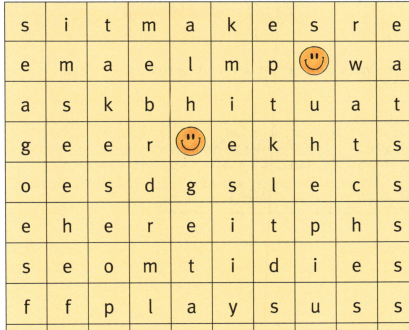

Some letters are left over. Find the sentence they spell.

My home

3

No, she doesn't.
No, he doesn't.   Yes, he does.   Yes, she does.

6 Quiz time

a) Can you answer these questions?

1 Does David play the guitar? _____
2 Does Gillian go to bed late on Saturdays? _____
3 Does Claire live in London? _____
4 Does Rajiv like maths lessons? _____
5 Does Gillian collect CDs? _____
6 Does Caroline help Rajiv with his new room? _____

b) Make four questions about the children from Camden Market for a partner. Can he/she answer them?

7 Four rooms

Read A3 in your textbook at page 50 again. Draw lines to the people.

1 "Our rooms are small, but they're very tidy."
2 "My room is not very big, but it has got two beds."
3 "We don't do our homework in our bedrooms."
4 "My room is quiet, so I do my homework there."
5 "I often put my clothes on the floor."
6 "We haven't got a toilet in our flat."
7 "Our flat is very small and noisy."
8 "We sometimes read ghost stories in bed."

Rick   Brad   Anna and Sofia   Ricco and Sandra

8 Do you …?

a) Work with a partner. Write down eight questions with *Do you …?* Then ask your partner and tick (✓) the right boxes.

Do you

collect
eat
help
like
play
read
watch
wear

animals • books in bed • coins • comics • earrings • English
football • fruit • glasses • going to the market • hamburgers
jeans • model cars • movies • sandwiches • skirts
stamps • swimming • the guitar • TV • with the cleaning
with the shopping • your mum • …

Yes, I do.
No, I don't.

	Yes	No		Yes	No
1 _____	☐	☐	5 _____	☐	☐
2 _____	☐	☐	6 _____	☐	☐
3 _____	☐	☐	7 _____	☐	☐
4 _____	☐	☐	8 _____	☐	☐

b) Now write about your partner. You can start like this: <u>My partner's name is Yasmin. She likes chocolate, but she doesn't like milk.</u>

_____
_____
_____

9 What about YOU?

 Do exercises a) and b).   Do exercises b) and c).

a) Write the words in the grid and talk about yourself. You can add more words, too.

> hockey   fish   blue eyes   English   spaghetti   boys
> cards   girls   basketball   school   table tennis   ice cream   mice
> skirts   ...   chocolate cake   Mondays   posters   coffee

😊 I play	😞 I don't play	😊 I eat	😞 I don't eat	😊 I like	😞 I don't like	😊 I've got	😞 I haven't got

b) What about Gillian? What does/doesn't she play/eat/like? What has/hasn't she got?
Write eight sentences in your exercise book.

LiF 4, 14R, 16

c) What about YOU?
Write six sentences in your exercise book.

> play • eat • like • have got

My home

3

10 A spooky party

Was or *were*? Read about the ghosts' party and cross out the wrong words.

LiF 22

Last night Spook was / ~~were~~ very excited. He was / were at Mrs MacHowl's party at her hotel. There was / were lots of guests at the party. Two of the guests was / were poltergeists from Germany. One of the German ghosts was / were Miss Griff and the other was / were Miss Mut. They was / were very spooky. But the star guest at Mrs MacHowl's party was / were Spook's friend, Nessie, a Scottish monster. There was / were only a little problem. Nessie was / were very friendly and very funny, but she was / were also very big and very hungry. Soon there was / were no food left for the other guests – it was / were all in Nessie's stomach!

Draw a picture of this story.

11 Last year in Scotland

LiF 22

a) Read the story on page 52 in your textbook again. Give short answers.

1 Were Joe and Mo ghosts from Germany? _____

2 Was Mrs MacHowl afraid of the poltergeists? _____

3 Was the bedroom for the two poltergeists warm and comfortable? _____

4 Was Mrs MacHowl friendly to her guests? _____

5 Were Miss Griff and Miss Mut from London? _____

b) Ask questions with a question word and *was/were*.

1 __What was__ the ghost story in your textbook about? (what?)
  The story was about Mrs MacHowl's spooky hotel.

2 _____ Mo and Joe in Scotland? (when?)
  Mo and Joe were in Scotland last year.

3 _____ the guests from Germany? (who?)
  Miss Griff and Miss Mut were the guests from Germany.

4 _____ it warm in the living room? (why?)
  Because there was a fire.

12 Rooms

WORDBANK F
houses

Can you find the words?

1 We usually make our meals in the CHIKENT. _____

2 You are lucky to have a ROBEMOD just for you. _____

3 When you're dirty, you need the OMABORTH. _____

4 You can see Grandma Williams' GIVLIN MOOR on TB page 47. _____

5 In big houses, people have their meals in the GINNID ROMO. _____

6 The LOTTIE is usually a small room, but without it – Oh, dear! _____

13 Jobs at home

a) Fill in *sometimes, often, normally*.

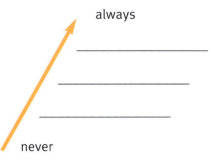

always
_____
_____
_____
never

b) What about you? How often do YOU do these things? Use *normally, often, never, always, sometimes*.

1 I make breakfast for my family. _____
2 I do the washing up.   _____
3 I write emails.   _____
4 I go to school on Sundays.   _____
5 I go shopping.   _____

14 Who does what?

a) Write about YOUR family.

WHO
- cleans the living room?
- feeds the pets?
- makes your bed?
- makes breakfast on Sundays?
- washes up?
- does the shopping?
- cleans the kitchen?
- cleans the windows?
- cleans the floor?
- tidies up your room?

I always feed the pets. I don't do the shopping.

My brother cleans the windows. My mum doesn't …

_____
_____
_____
_____

TIP
Use simple present if you are clever with, always, often, somtimes, never.

b) Who does what in your family? Talk about their jobs.

My father washes up.

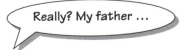
Really? My father …

My home

3

LiF 4R, 17R

15 Subject – adverb – verb – object

Put the words in the right order. Then write down the sentences.

1 [3] do [5] on Saturdays [1] The Butlers [4] the shopping [2] usually
The Butlers usually do the shopping on Saturdays.

2 [ ] helps [ ] his parents [ ] in the shop [ ] often [ ] Rajiv
_____

3 [ ] after breakfast [ ] always [ ] David [ ] feeds [ ] Hoover
_____

4 [ ] Caroline and Gillian [ ] cook [ ] for their families [ ] meals [ ] sometimes
_____

5 [ ] Charlie and David [ ] make [ ] never [ ] the beds
_____

6 [ ] always [ ] does [ ] Grandma Williams [ ] on Mondays [ ] the washing
_____

16 Rhyming words

Find the rhyming words and colour them in nine different colours.

MAKE HOUSE STAY BLUE CAKE CHAIR TEA MAN ME GREY NEW BOOK NOISE HAIR CAN WHO SAY MOUSE LOOK BOYS YOU SHE TAKE TOYS SEE FAIR DAY TWO WHERE

My home 3

17 Our favourite places

Use the sentences to complete the puzzle. What is the solution?

1. The paths along the canal are full of beautiful ... in summer.
2. Caroline loves the ... cafés on the canal.
3. ... is a football team.
4. The ... in Primrose Hill Park are good for inline skaters.
5. Your textbook is called Camden ...
6. Caroline likes the paths along the ...
7. Caroline often meets her ... in the cafés on the canal.
8. Caroline likes to eat ice cream at a ...
9. David is in the snooker club at his ...
10. David enjoys football, ... and snooker.
11. There are more ... in Regent's Park than in Primrose Hill Park.
12. Inline ... like the paths because there are not so many people there.

Camden Market

Grand Union Canal

Primrose Hill Park

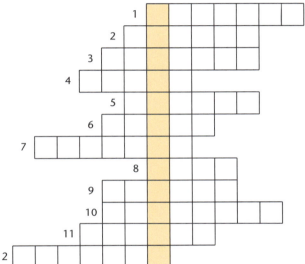

The solution is: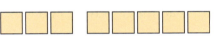

TIP
Read C1 in your TB at page 57 again for help.

18 Oh, no!

Complete the text with verbs from the box.

eat • go • hates • help • love • meet • need • sit • stay • watch • welcome • work

It's Saturday, and the friends want to ___meet___ in Camden. But where? Rajiv must help his parents. "You must _____ here today, Rajiv," Mr Khan says. "We _____ you in the shop. But your friends are always _____ here."

"Oh, no," Caroline says. "It's a beautiful day. I don't want to _____ in a room behind a shop! I want to ____ to the canal." "Right," says Gillian. "We can _____ an ice cream in a café, and then we can go to Primrose Hill Park." "Cool," Emma says. "We can _____ the inline skaters there."

"Oh, no," David says. "Hoover _____ inline skaters, and they hate him. Dogs and inline skaters? No, thank you! And what about poor Rajiv? He has to _____." "You're right," Charlie says. "I know. The girls can go to the canal and the park, and we can _____ Rajiv in the shop. I _____ free food!"

My town

19 Places in Camden

CD

a) Ron and Julie are at Camden Road Station.
Listen and look at the map.

Where do they want to go?

_____

TIP
You can follow the directions with a pencil.

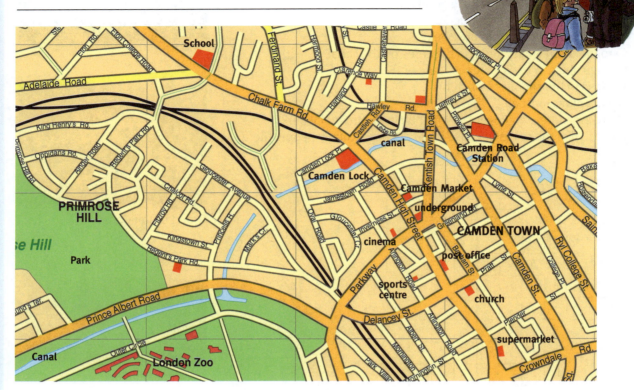

b) Read the directions and look at the map. Where do the people want to go?

> We want to go to _____. Can you tell us the way, please?

Oh, that's easy. See, you are at Camden Road Station. Walk down Parkway, turn into the third street on the right. That's Camden High Street. Go straight and then it's on the first street on your right.

> Can you tell me the way to _____, please?

Let's see, we are in front of Camden Lock Market. Just go straight. Walk under that train brigde there. The street is called Chalk Farm Road then. Just keep straight. It's opposite Adelaide Road. But I don't think it's open today. It's Sunday.

☾ **c)** You are at Camden Lock. Look at the map and describe the way to …

… the post office

Go to Camden High Street. Turn …
_____
_____

… the cinema
_____
_____

38

☼ d) Which place in Camden do you like best? Why?

_____

_____

_____

20 Things to do

What can you do in YOUR town or area? Find the pairs. Draw lines.

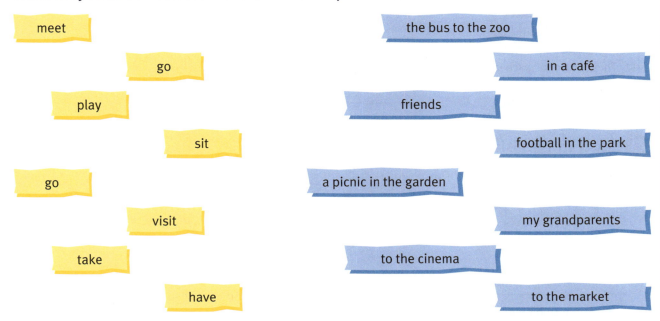

meet		the bus to the zoo
go		in a café
play		friends
sit		football in the park
go	a picnic in the garden	
visit		my grandparents
take		to the cinema
have		to the market

21 In my neighbourhood

a) Make a mindmap about your neighbourhood.

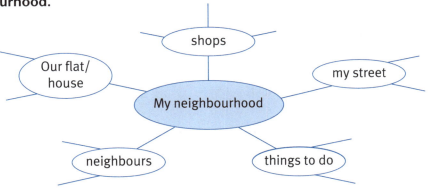

Mindmap: My neighbourhood — shops, Our flat/house, my street, neighbours, things to do

TOOLBOX F
How to ... write

WORDBANK G
towns

b) Now write about your neighbourhood. What do/don't you like? What can/can't you do there?

_____

_____

_____

_____

My town

22 Say and write

What are the long forms?

You say:	You write:
I'm Emma Butler.	_____
Hoover's in the park.	_____
Where's Rajiv?	_____
Charlie's a very good footballer.	_____
We're all in the same class.	_____
They're twelve years old.	_____
It's a beautiful day.	_____

23 Say it in English

Was sagst du auf Englisch, wenn ...

1 ... du in Urlaub bist?
_____

2 ... dir etwas Leid tut?
_____

3 ... du jemanden kennen lernst?
_____

4 ... du vor etwas Angst hast?
_____

5 ... du nach dem Weg fragen willst?
_____

6 ... du jemandem den Weg beschreiben willst?
_____

7 ... du ein Möbelstück bequem findest?
_____

8 ... etwas viel Arbeit ist?
_____

9 ... du jemandem einen Tipp für deine Stadt geben willst?
_____

10 ... jemand leise sein soll?
_____

- Go straight on. It's the second on the left.
- Can you tell me the way to ..., please?
- It's a lot of work.
- This armchair is very comfortable.
- I'm afraid of big dogs.
- I'm on holiday.
- Nice to meet you.
- Be quiet, please.
- I'm sorry.
- The best place in my town is ...

At home

👉 Test yourself 👈

Du bist nun ja schon mit den *Test yourself*-Seiten vertraut. Bearbeite sie wie in den letzten beiden *Themes*. Vergiss nicht, anschließend den Portfolio-Fragebogen auszufüllen.

1 Listening: Kenny's room

Listen to Kenny. Put the furniture in the right place in his room. Draw lines.

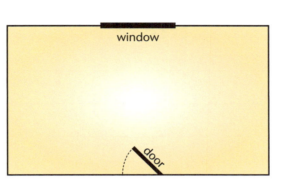

2 Reading: Tom's dream room

Read about Tom's dream room and look at the picture. Find the wrong words and correct the text.

My dream room

My dream room has a ~~football goal~~ **basketball basket** so that I can play football every day. It is a big room. There are pink crocodiles on the wall – my favourite animals. There is a shelf for my crocodiles, too. I haven't got a desk. I keep my pens and pencils in my wardrobe. I have got a poster with my favourite pop singer on it. He has got a blue T-shirt and black hair. I have got a new radio so I can listen to rap music. I love hip hop! I can watch TV in my room, too.

3 Speaking: Giving directions

Look at the street plan on pages 58 and 59 of your textbook. You are at Camden Market. A boy asks you for directions. Help him. He wants to go to:

Camden Road Station

Go along ... Street/Road.
Go straight on.
Go across the canal/...
Turn left/right into ...
It's the first/second/third street on the right/left.
The station/zoo... is opposite/next to/in ...

_____

_____

_____

At home

4 Writing: My room

Write an email to an English friend about your room.

> My new room is ...
> There is/are ... in/on/under/next to/behind/in front of/opposite the ...
> in the corner, on the floor, on the wall(s), next to/under the window, behind/opposite the door, ...

Hi,

_____

_____

_____

_____

_____

_____

CU,

_____

5 Grammar: An interview

Look at Gillian's answers. Make questions with *do* or *does*.

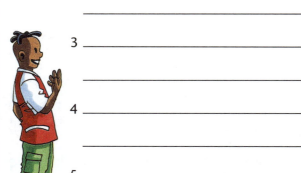

1 _____

2 _____

3 _____

4 _____

5 _____

1 No, I live with my mum. My dad lives in Notting Hill with his new family.

2 No, I don't eat meat. I only eat vegetables and spaghetti and fruit, of course.

3 No, my cat doesn't like dogs. But she likes mice!

4 Yes, I always make my bed. My mum says I have to.

5 Oh yes, my grandma always forgets things.

What I can say

4

1 Animal quiz

⭐ Can you find four animals?
Colour them and write about them.

My animal number 1 is a _____ (colour) _____ (animal).

_____

_____

_____

🌙☀️ Find the names for the drawings. Then write sentences.

① cat ③ elephant ⑥ snake rabbit cow ⑦ penguin ⑧ dog ④ ⑤ parrot

LiF 5R

Number 1 is _____

Number 2 is _____

_____

_____

_____

_____

_____

_____

2 Zoo noises

Listen to the children at the zoo.
What animals are they looking at?

1 _____

2 _____

3 _____

4 _____

5 _____

CD

snakes   hippos   elephants   lions   tigers   monkeys   penguins   crocodiles   spiders

3 Pets

a) Listen to the children again. Tick (✓) if the sentences about their pets are true or false.

		true	false
1	Hannibal eats a lot of meat.	☐	✓
2	Hannibal loves carrots and cucumbers.	☐	☐
3	David's pet is black and white and aggressive.	☐	☐
4	David's pet sleeps in a basket in the hall.	☐	☐
5	Ben's pet lives in a glass cage.	☐	☐
6	Ben's pet sleeps all day.	☐	☐
7	Gillian's pet likes dogs.	☐	☐
8	Gillian's pet never eats mice.	☐	☐
9	Lucy's pet is green and blue and lives in a cage.	☐	☐
10	Lucy's pet can't talk.	☐	☐

b) Now write the correct sentences.

Hannibal eats fruit and vegetables.

_____

_____

_____

_____

_____

4 Who knows?

a) Draw lines and sort the words in the sorting machine into adjectives, nouns and verbs.

clever clean basket sleep funny tall water look for pet thin meat puppy run drink sweet fly grey kitten fruit friendly call shop fast soft expensive play eat vegetable touch fish

Adjectives   Nouns   Verbs

b) Write sentences with two words from each list in your exercise book.

5 Pet food

a) What can these animals (not) eat?

can / can't eat …

is / isn't / are / aren't good for …

Lemonade isn't good for fish.

_____

_____

_____

_____

_____

b) Work with a partner. Ask and answer questions.

Is ice cream good for cats? — *Yes, it is.* — *No, it isn't.*

6 Sounds

a) Write down the past tense forms. Then read them out loud.

[-d]	[-t]	[-ɪd]
dance____	watch____	start____
play____	walk____	need____
learn____	talk____	collect____
listen____	like____	wait____
clean____	work____	hate____
____	____	____
____	____	____

b) What are the past tense forms of these verbs? Write them in the correct list.

look • want • live • cook • love • paint

c) Can you find a rule for the [-ɪd] words?

TOOLBOX H
How to … work with grammar

Pets
4
LiF 1R, 7R, 9R

LiF 23

45

Pets

7 Butterfly's Tuesday afternoon

Gillian's afternoon at the pet shop was very exciting. Her cat had an interesting afternoon, too. Can you tell Butterfly's story?

walk in the garden

wash my face

watch a dog

look at birds

wait for you in my basket

talk to Fuzzy, the neighbour's cat

play with a ball

"Well, Gillian, my afternoon was really nice. First …"

_____
_____
_____
_____
_____
_____

8 Dog friends

Hoover's friends want to know what happened in the park. They have got a lot of questions. Write their questions.

1   **Blackie:** (what/hear)
    What did you hear?   **Hoover:** A girl shouted for help.

2   **Luna:** (what/do)
    _____? **Hoover:** I looked at the pond.

3   **Blackie:** _____?   **Hoover:** There was a girl in the water. She was
    (what/see)   afraid of an angry big black dog.

4   **Luna:** _____?   **Hoover:** Grrr! Grrr! All my friends are here in the
    (what/tell/the dog)   park. They can bite you! Woof!

5   **Blackie:** _____?   **Hoover:** Yes, he did. He didn't wait for my friends!
    (the dog/run away)

6   **Luna:** _____?   **Hoover:** She was too cold to speak.
    (what/girl/say)

7   **Blackie:** _____?   **Hoover:** A very, very big ice cream!
    (what/David/give)

8   **Luna:** _____?   **Hoover:** Yes, but we didn't stay. I don't like to
    (police/come)   answer questions – woof!

9 At the police

David went to the police the next day. Write down short answers with *was/were* and *did*.

 **Policewoman:** **David:**

1 David, you were at Primrose Hill Park yesterday, right?   Yes, I was.

2 Was a black and white dog with you?   _____

3 Were you and your dog near the pond?   _____

4 Did you hear a girl shout for help?   _____

5 Did your dog pull the girl to the bank?   _____

6 Did your dog run after the big black dog?   _____

7 Did you read about your dog in the newspaper?   _____

10 Spook

Spook's mother is at home again after a holiday. She is very angry because Spook didn't do any of his jobs. What does she say?

Dear Spooky-Boy,
Please:
– buy bread and tea
– clean the floor
– wash up the dirty cups
– cook my favourite spider meal
– tidy up the kitchen
Love, Mum

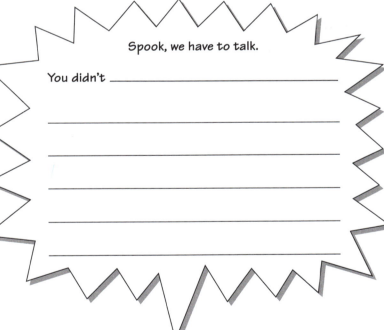

Spook, we have to talk.
You didn't _____

But I didn't forget to visit my friend Nessie!

Draw a picture of his mother's face.

Pets

4

11 The hedgehog story

Put the sentences into the right order. Read out the two parts of the story.

In Regent's Park (1)

1	Charlie, Rajiv and Gillian were in Regent's Park.
	Gillian took the hedgehog home in a box.
	He got the hedgehog and showed it to Gillian and Charlie.
3	Rajiv ran to the road and stopped a motorbike.
	Rajiv said snails, Charlie said milk and Gillian said "Ugh!"
5	The three friends talked about what food to give the hedgehog.
	They saw a hedgehog on the road.

TIP
Look in your textbook at page 73 for help.

At Gillian's house (2)

5	But Mrs Collins said "No." She said, "Give her some water and an apple."
3	But Mrs Collins wasn't interested. She said, "No wild animals in the house!"
	"But then take it back to the park," she said.
	Gillian didn't like the idea. "Oh no, Mum", she said.
	Gillian said the hedgehog wasn't an 'it', but a 'she' – Henrietta.
	Then Gillian asked her mother for some milk for Henrietta.
1	When Mrs Collins saw the hedgehog, she said, "You can't bring it into the house."

12 A hedgehog at school?

Fill in the right words.

LiF 19R

him • her (2x) • us • them • you • me • it

Teacher: Gillian, what have you got in that box?

Gillian: It's a hedgehog. Her name is Henrietta and she's from Regent's Park. Can't I bring _____ to school? Please let _____ stay.

Teacher: A hedgehog is a wild animal. You can't bring _____ into the classroom.

Gillian: But Henrietta is clean and friendly.

Teacher: No, Gillian, Henrietta can stay with _____ now. Just put the box on my desk. But you have to take _____ back to the park after school. Rajiv can help _____. Ask _____ – or the girls over there. You can ask _____, too.

Gillian: OK. Be nice to Mr Graham, Henrietta.

Wild animals

13 What's the word in English?

a) Here is a puzzle about a wild animal. Can you fill in the English words? You can look at the German-English dictionary in your textbook for help.

This animal is NOT _____ (**freundlich**). It is _____ (**gefährlich**) and most people

_____ (**haben Angst**) of this _____ (**furchtbares**) animal. It is very

_____ (**stark**) and can run very _____ (**schnell**). It eats _____

(**Fleisch**) and it sometimes eats people too. This animal lives in cold _____ (**Länder**). In Russia,

_____ (**zum Beispiel**).

It is a | w | | | |

TOOLBOX E
How to ... work with a dictionary

b) Use the English-German dictionary in your textbook to find out the meaning of these words.

lizard – _____   leaf – _____   nibble – _____

tail – _____   nature – _____

14 Another tiger story

a) This is a limerick, 'The young lady of Riga', but the lines are mixed up. Can you find the correct order?

☐ And the smile¹ on the face of the tiger.
☒ 1 There was a young lady from Riga
☐ They returned² from the ride³
☐ Who rode with a smile on a tiger.
☐ With the lady inside

¹smile – *Lächeln*   ²return – *zurückkommen*   ³ride – *Ritt*

_____

_____

_____

_____

_____

b) Now listen to the limerick on the CD. Did you get it right?

49

Wild animals

4 | 15 Verbs, verbs, verbs

⭐ Find pairs. Draw lines.

touch — touched
pull — pulled
jump — jumped
shout — shouted
have — had
took — take (connected)
catch — caught
happen — happened
give — gave
see — saw
eat — ate

☀ Find twenty verbs in puzzle A. Then find the simple past forms in puzzle B.
In puzzle B there is one new simple past form – what is it?

A

E	A	T	A	C	O	M	E	B	T
G	I	V	E	A	F	E	N	O	O
B	W	M	O	X	Y	E	J	K	U
N	A	S	T	A	Y	T	O	R	C
M	L	P	J	P	L	A	Y	I	H
P	K	L	U	V	T	H	I	N	K
L	Q	O	M	A	K	E	F	U	I
I	S	O	P	E	N	V	S	A	Y
V	Z	K	T	A	K	E	E	Z	O
E	F	U	L	O	V	E	E	U	P

B

T	O	O	K	H	T	S	A	I	D
W	E	N	T	J	U	M	P	E	D
E	N	J	O	Y	E	D	L	G	H
L	I	V	E	D	T	O	A	T	T
L	O	V	E	D	A	P	Y	O	H
S	T	A	Y	E	D	E	E	U	O
S	G	C	A	M	E	N	D	C	U
A	A	L	O	O	K	E	D	H	G
W	V	J	K	M	A	D	E	E	H
M	E	T	W	A	L	K	E	D	T

regular verbs

infinitive — simple past

irregular verbs

infinitive — simple past

Wild animals 4

 Circle the odd one out.

1. ate – went – want – slept – thought
2. knew – gave – threw – new – saw
3. tried – helped – lived – loved – excited
4. brought – found – loud – caught – thought
5. walked – had – cooked – worked – asked
6. feel – get – did – be – try

Find the simple past forms of these verbs in the list of irregular verbs on the last page of your workbook.

take – _____ | fly – _____ | leave – _____ | can – _____

16 Last Friday

a) Last Friday, Charlie's mother went out with her friends. She asked Charlie to do some jobs. Listen to Charlie and his mother. Did Charlie do all his jobs on Friday? Tick (✔) yes or no.

Charlie: Your jobs. Don't forget!!
– take eggs to Mrs White
– tidy up your room
– call Gran
– feed hamster
– go shopping
  (read shopping list!)

yes no
☐ ☐
☐ ☐
☐ ☐
☐ ☐
☐ ☐

b) Which jobs did Charlie do? Which jobs didn't he do?

_____

_____

_____

 Write his mother's questions and Charlie's answers in your exercise book.
Mother: Did you ...? **Charlie:** I took ...

☀ What jobs did YOU do yesterday? What didn't you do? Write five sentences in your exercise book.

17 Run-away tiger

There is an article about a run-away tiger in the newspaper. Fill in the simple past forms.

Run-away tiger

London. Yesterday afternoon a tiger (run) _____ away from London Zoo. It (walk) _____ in the streets of London. The keeper* (go) _____ to the cage at 5.30pm but the tiger (be) _____ not there. The keeper (call) _____ the police. The news about the tiger (be) _____ on the radio. Many people (be) _____ frightened because a tiger is a wild and dangerous animal. They (call) _____ the police hotline. Finally the police (find) _____ the tiger in Kensington Gardens near the Round Pond. It (be) _____ very sleepy. They (catch) _____ it and (bring) _____ it back to the zoo.

*Tierpfleger

Wild animals

4

18 Story time

Match the sentence parts. The letters in B make a word.

A

1 After his afternoon meal, the tiger …
2 He found the key to his cage …
3 The tiger swam in a canal but he …
4 He wanted to say hello to people in the park …
5 The tiger tried to buy a ticket to Madame Tussaud's …
6 He was so hungry that he …
7 The tiger ate the sandwich …
8 Then he was tired so he slept in …

B

(u) … and opened the door.
(o) … and then he looked at the shops.
(n) … a park, where the police caught him.
(i) … asked a tourist for his sandwich.
(t) … but they didn't let him in.
(s) … but they were frightened and ran away.
(e) … didn't enjoy it because the water was dirty.
(q) … wanted to walk around London.

The word is ☐☐☐☐☐☐☐☐

19 Why?

Read B6 on page 76 of your textbook again and answer the questions.

1 Why did the tiger run away from the zoo?

   Because he wanted to walk around London.

2 Why didn't he like swimming in the canal?

   _____

3 Why did the tiger go to Madame Tussaud's?

   _____

4 Why did the tiger eat a tourist's sandwich?

   _____

5 Why did he sleep in Kensington Gardens?

   _____

Farm animals

20 At Kentish Town Farm

a) Look at the woman at the information point. Here are her answers. Write the correct letter next to the question in the picture.

- A Piglets? Yes, of course. Over there, near the trees.
- B No, sorry, you can't.
- C Go straight on, turn right.
- D There's a snack bar in the farmhouse.
- E Yes, do you want one?

b) Listen to the song 'Old McDonald'. Write down the names of the animals.

_____   _____   _____   _____   _____

Farm animals

4

21 A crossword puzzle

**Fill in the words in the crossword puzzle.
What is the solution?**

WORDBANK
animals

Clues

Jessie isn't only a ①. She's a sheepdog.

You can see ② in the photo on page 82 in the textbook.

Dogs can't speak, but they can ③.

After lunch, the ④ made angry sounds.

⑤ say 'quack quack'.

A sheepdog with ⑥ barked at Emma and Jack.

Emma and Jack tried to stroke the ⑦, but they didn't like strangers.

Grandma was on Mumbo, a lovely ⑧ pony.

Animals like friends, but they don't like ⑨.

Mumbo and Jumbo are ⑩.

Grandma took a funny ⑪ of Emma and Jack in the bog.

The Butlers' farm is a ⑫ farm.

22 Emma and Jack's holiday

**Read the speech bubbles
and say who is talking.**

Emma
Emma and Jack
Jack (2x)
Grandma
Grandpa
Mr Butler

TIP
Read C2 on pages 80–81 in your textbook to check your answers.

① I can carry my bag, thanks, Grandpa. I'm not a baby.

② You can have a lot of fun on a farm, kids.

③ Let me carry your bags for you.

④ The moors can be dangerous. Take Jessie with you and don't go off the road.

⑤ Yes, but they live on the moors. There are no shops, Dad!

⑥ They don't know us. We're strangers here, Jack.

⑦ Why are the hens angry? Why does the dog bark at us? They're stupid!

23 Say it in English

Was sagst du, wenn du …

What did you do yesterday? Careful!
How much is a ticket, please? I love vegetables. Go on, please.

1 … Gemüse gerne magst?

_____

2 … fragen willst, was jemand gestern gemacht hat?

_____

3 … möchtest, dass jemand weiter erzählt?

_____

4 … nach dem Preis fragen willst?

_____

5 … jemanden warnen willst?

_____

54

☞ Test yourself ☜

Bearbeite die *Test yourself*-Seiten wie in den letzten *Themes*. Vergiss nicht, anschließend den Portfolio-Fragebogen auszufüllen.

1 Listening: Our pets

Listen to the five children. What are their pets? Write them in the boxes.

1	2	3	4	5
____	____	____	____	____

2 Reading: Penguins or elephants?

Read about the animals and complete the information box.

Penguins
There are seventeen kinds of penguins all over the world. The penguins at London Zoo are Jackass Penguins from South Africa. People really like to watch them because they are very sweet. And they have got a funny walk. Penguins can't fly like birds but they are very good swimmers. They 'fly' through the water. When their keeper* feeds them fish, they walk after him. Jackass Penguins are between 68 and 70 cm tall. Many baby penguins are born in London Zoo.

Elephants
Elephants are very strong and clever animals. They come from Africa and Asia. In Asia elephants work hard in camps. The keepers at London Zoo wash and feed their big friends and they clean their teeth and feet. The elephants eat a lot of hay** and drink a lot of water. The keepers take the elephants for long walks around the zoo. And sometimes the keepers sit on their backs.

*Tierpfleger   **Heu

	Penguins	**Elephants**
1 Where do they come from?		
2 What do they eat?		
3 What do they do?	(2 things)	(1 thing)
4 What do the keepers do?	(1 thing)	(2 things)

3 Words: Odd one out

Circle the odd one out.

1 carrot – milk – cucumber – eat – bread
2 happen – swim – carry – pull – jump
3 thin – soft – strange – arrive – sharp
4 angry – sad – rain – excited – aggressive
5 road – street – canal – park – fast
6 farm – cow – shout – flat – cage

Pets

4 Speaking: What do these sentences tell you?

Look at the sentences. Decide if they …

- describe something   A
- are from a story   B
- tell you what to do   C

Write the correct letter in the box.

They eat snails and drink water.

Then he swam in the canal and walked in the park.

Clean her cage every week.

He ran away from the zoo.

It has got beautiful soft fur.

Don't give her milk.

5 Writing: Emma's postcard

Write Emma's postcard to Caroline from the Yorkshire Moors.

Hi Caroline,

We are here for two weeks. The moors are _____

_____

The farm animals _____

_____

A stupid thing happened yesterday. We went _____

_____

_____

But Grandma found us. She _____

_____

I want to be home in Camden soon!!
                                                Emma

6 Grammar: Simple past

The lion tells the other animals at the zoo about his life in Africa.
Fill in the simple past forms.

Many years ago, before I (come) _____ to London Zoo, I (live) _____ in

Africa – and I (be) _____ free! I (be) _____ the king of the animals and

I (have) _____ a big family. I often (run) _____ for two or three hours

and then I (catch) _____ an animal for my meal – always fresh food! Then I (go)

_____ to the river and (swim) _____ a little bit. After that I (feel)

_____ really tired and I (sleep) _____ under a big tree. In the evening

I (play) _____ and (talk) _____ to all the other lions. What a life!

1 At Camden Café

a) Listen to the dialogue. Which words can you hear? Tick (✓) the right boxes.

apple ☐	chocolate ☐	milk ☐
bread ☐	cola ☐	sandwich ☐
cake ☐	egg ☐	steak ☐
chicken ☐	fish ☐	water ☐

b) What do you think of when you hear the words 'food and drink'? Make a mindmap.

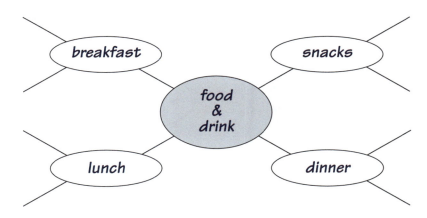

2 A picture dictionary

Look at these pictures. What are the English words? Make a picture dictionary. You can use the German-English dictionary in your textbook for help.

What I can say 5

CD

TOOLBOX B
How to ... work with words

TIP
Cut out more pictures from brochures.

_____   _____   _____

_____   _____   _____

_____   _____   _____

Shopping

5

3 Ken's fruit stall

Annie Snow wants to buy some apples from Ken's fruit stall. Put the speech bubbles in the right order from 1 to 9.

☐ Fine. Here you are. Four green apples.

☐ Goodbye.

1 Hello. I'd like four apples, please. The green ones.

☐ How much is that, please?

☐ OK. Here's £1.50.

☐ Thank you, and here's your change. Bye now.

☐ That's £1.20, please.

WORDBANK J
shopping

4 Say it in English

Was sagst du, wenn …

1 … du Bananen kaufen möchtest?
_____

2 … du kein Kleingeld hast?
_____

3 … etwas kein Problem ist?
_____

4 … du das Wechselgeld zurückgibst?
_____

5 … du nach dem Preis fragst?
_____

6 … du jemandem einen schönen Tag wünschst?
_____

7 … du auf der Suche nach einem T-Shirt bist?
_____

8 … dir etwas zu teuer ist?
_____

I'm looking for a T-shirt.

Here's your change.

I've only got £10. Is that OK?

Have a nice day.

That's no problem.

That's too expensive for me.

How much is/are …?

Hello. I'd like three bananas, please.

5 George, the market seller

George is selling some of his things. A little boy wants to buy something, but he can't read. He wants to know the prices.

Write George's answers. Watch out for *this/that* and *these/those*.

... the posters?   This poster is £2, that poster is 80p.

... the books?

... the videos?

... the caps?

... the pencil cases?

... the computer games?

... the T-shirts?

6 Sounds

What letters can't you hear? Circle (◯) them.

(k)now   write   tomorrow   wrong   night   arm   right

Shopping

LiF 27

TIP
HERE
this (= one)
these (= more than one)
THERE
that (= one)
those (=more than one)

CD

Shopping

5

7 The price of things

a) Colour the things and give them prices.

b) Ask your partner how much his/her things cost.

> How much are your purple jeans?

> They're …

> That's expensive! My red jeans are …

> That's cheap. What about your green shirt? How much is it?

> It's …

8 At the supermarket

Charlie and his sister Josephine are in a supermarket. Listen to the CD and write down the prices. Is the total correct?

ARTICLE	PRICE
milk	_____
chips	_____
apples	_____
chicken	_____
yoghurt	_____
cheese	_____
bread	_____
cornflakes	_____
sugar	_____
orange juice	_____
chocolate cake	_____
comic	_____
TOTAL	**£11.59**
PAID	**£15.00**
CHANGE	**£3.41**

Shopping 5

9 One thing, two things

a) Write the plurals of these words.

birthday   family   toy   knife   potato   foot
child   tomato   diary   Monday   story   box

-ies	-s	-es	!! (difficult)

b) Find more plurals. You can look at your word lists.

10 A present for David

Read A5 on page 95 of your textbook again.
Match the sentence parts to find the solution.

1 Rajiv is sitting at the table in the kitchen but …
2 He has got an invitation to …
3 After breakfast Rajiv goes to the market to …
4 Rajiv thinks carefully about a good present: …
5 Rajiv doesn't know what CD to buy, and …
6 Then Rajiv comes to a stall that …
7 At this stall, he finds …
8 Rajiv buys the poster and …

(t) … a CD, a book or perhaps a model?
(a) … a fantastic poster of a big white shark.
(r) … buy a birthday present for David.
(h) … David isn't interested in models.
(b) … he isn't eating his breakfast.
(y) … shows it to his friends.
(i) … his friend David's birthday party.
(d) … sells lots of exciting things.

The solution is

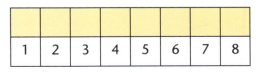

Birthdays

11 Are they ready?

It is quarter to three on Saturday afternoon. The Butler family has got an invitation to a birthday party at three o'clock. Is everybody ready?

Emma and her mother are in the bathroom. Mrs Butler is cleaning her  _____

and Emma is washing her _____. Jack, Emma's brother, is playing the

 _____. And Jack's friend is feeding the  _____.

Only Mr Butler is waiting in the  _____.

12 A birthday cake

Find the birthday words.

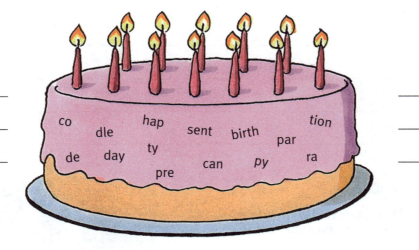

_____
_____
_____

_____
_____
_____

LiF 28

13 More about David's party

Work with a partner. Look at the photos and talk about David's party.

| having a great time | talking to | eating a lot of cake |
| going home | dancing | sitting on the sofa |

Rajiv is …   They are …

Birthdays

5

 What is wrong with these sentences? Look at the photos on page 62 and write correct sentences.

1 Rajiv is drinking a lot of coke. _____.

2 The guests are singing "Happy Birthday". _____.

3 Rajiv is sitting on the table. _____.

4 Caroline is talking to Mrs Williams. _____.

5 The guests are doing their homework. _____.

6 Caroline and Rajiv are eating cornflakes. _____.

Here are some more photos of the party. What is happening?

_____
_____
_____
_____
_____
_____

Birthdays

5

14 Word search

a) Find fifteen *-ing* forms in the word search.

A	G	N	I	K	A	T	Q	H	V	F	S
G	N	I	K	O	O	C	S	T	F	L	I
O	I	G	N	I	R	E	W	S	N	A	T
I	V	X	G	E	T	T	I	N	G	U	T
N	I	C	H	E	T	V	M	R	N	G	I
G	R	P	M	B	I	G	M	N	I	H	N
G	R	O	E	I	Q	G	I	B	C	I	G
M	A	K	I	N	G	O	N	D	N	N	N
X	P	U	T	T	I	N	G	T	A	G	M
E	G	N	R	T	G	N	I	O	D	I	J
Y	T	G	R	U	N	N	I	N	G	C	A
A	N	D	R	I	V	I	N	G	Y	E	T

b) Put the fifteen *-ing* forms into the right column.

double consonant (pu**t**, pu**tt**ing)	no -e (escape, escap**ing**)	-ing (help, help**ing**)

15 At seven o'clock at David's party

Look at the pictures and answer the questions.

TIP
still = immer noch

1 Is David still playing with his friends?

   No, he isn't. He is carrying his presents.

2 Is Uncle Morgan still dancing?

   _____

   _____

3 Are Aunt Fay and David's mother having tea?

   _____

   _____

4 Is David's father still making pizza?

   _____

   _____

64

16 David's family tree

a) Look at the family tree and the words. Then read the sentences about the family tree. Can you guess the meaning of the underlined words?

Gillian's parents are <u>divorced</u>. Gillian lives with her mother. Mrs Collins is a <u>single parent</u>.
Ivor Williams and Janet Williams are <u>married</u>. They have got three children together.
Thomas Williams is Alice Williams' <u>husband</u>. Alice is Thomas' wife.
Gillian is Fay Williams' <u>niece</u>, David is her <u>nephew</u>. Fay is David and Gillian's <u>aunt</u>. Her husband Morgan is their uncle.

daughter – son
grandmother – grandfather
mother – father
sister – brother
aunt – uncle
granddaughter – grandson
wife – husband
cousin – cousin
niece – nephew
parents – single parent
married – divorced

Ivor Williams 13/09   Janet Williams 17/12

Fay Williams 14/11   Morgan Williams 20/08   Gwen Collins 21/04   Paul Collins 31/05   Thomas Williams 31/12   Alice Williams 18/10

Gillian Collins 14/02   David Williams 15/04

Add the German words.

divorced – _____   married – _____   aunt – _____

husband – _____   nephew – _____

niece – _____   single parent – _____

b) Look at the Williams' family tree and tick (✓) the right boxes.

Example: Gwen is David's   ☐ mother   ☐ sister   ✓ a(u)nt   (2nd letter)

1 David is Ivor's	☐ son	☐ uncle	☐ grandson	(5th letter)
2 Ivor is Gwen's	☐ father	☐ aunt	☐ uncle	(2nd letter)
3 Thomas is Gillian's	☐ cousin	☐ uncle	☐ father	(1st letter)
4 Janet is Gillian's	☐ mother	☐ aunt	☐ grandmother	(1st letter)
5 Thomas is Morgan's	☐ son	☐ cousin	☐ brother	(5th letter)
6 Gwen is Thomas'	☐ cousin	☐ sister	☐ uncle	(4th letter)
7 Gillian is Gwen's	☐ sister	☐ daughter	☐ aunt	(7th letter)
8 Janet is Morgan's	☐ mother	☐ grandmother	☐ sister	(6th letter)

Can you find out the answer?

1	2	3	4	5	6	7	8

Birthdays

5

TIP
Check page 227 in your textbook for a list of numbers.

17 Days and months

a) Fill in the right words.

The (ninth/nine) _____ month is September.

June is the (sixth/six) _____ month.

The (fifth/five) _____ month is May.

There are (twenty-ninth/twenty-nine) _____ days in February every four years.

The last day of November is the (thirtieth/thirty) _____.

The 31st December is the (last/first) _____ day of the year.

December is the (twelfth/twelve) _____ month.

August is the (eighth/eight) _____ month.

The first day of the year is the (first/one) _____ of January.

October has (thirty-first/thirty-one) _____ days.

b) Three months are missing in a). Write them down.

_____   _____   _____

18 Birthdays

When are their birthdays? Write down the dates.

My birthday is on the twenty-first day of the year.
21st January

My birthday is on the second day of the fifth month.
_____

My birthday is on the last day of the eighth month.
_____

My birthday is on the fifteenth day of the eleventh month.
_____

My birthday is on the thirty-first day of the last month.
_____

My birthday is on the fourth day of the sixth month.
_____

My birthday is on the fifty-third day of the year.
_____

Birthdays

5

19 YOUR party

a) Answer the questions. The pictures can give you some ideas.

When is your birthday? _My birthday is_ _____

Who are your guests? _My guests are_ _____

What do you do? _We_ _____
_____
_____

What do you eat and drink? _____
_____
_____

Where do you go? _____
_____
_____
_____
_____

b) Now work with a partner. Ask him/her about his/her birthday. Write down the answers.

_____'s birthday is _____

Her/his guests are _____
_____

They _____
_____
_____
_____

Birthdays

20 A birthday tongue twister

Can you say this?

When is Aunt Ethel's birthday?
It's on Thursday.
It's on the thirtieth of May.
She will be thirty-three that day.
I'll go there with my brother,
With my father and my mother.
Aunt Ethel is my father's sister
That's the end of this tongue-twister.

21 Birthday poems

Read the poems and write a birthday poem for a friend.

The Birthday Cow
Happy Mooday to you
Happy Mooday to you
Happy Mooday
Dear Yooday
Happy Mooday to you

MELANIE, I WISH YOU
EASY TESTS
LOVELY WEATHER
ALL THE BEST
NICE THINGS
INTERESTING FRIENDS
EXCITING PRESENTS

birthday
nice cards
great presents
good music
happy friends
birthday

_____
_____
_____
_____
_____
_____

Test yourself

Bearbeite die *Test yourself*-Seiten wie in den letzten *Themes*. Du kannst mit einer Partnerin/einem Partner zusammenarbeiten, um eure Ergebnisse zu vergleichen. Wenn du anschließend deinen Portfolio-Fragebogen ausfüllst, überlege, welche Aufgaben dir leicht gefallen sind ☺, welche nicht ganz so einfach waren 😐 und welche du schwierig fandest ☹.

1 Listening: Dates

Listen to Charlie and tick (✓) the dates you hear.

14th February ☐   30th April ☐   14th July ☐   15th April ☐

21st May ☐   31st January ☐   2nd September ☐

23rd November ☐   8th February ☐   22nd June ☐

2 Reading: Spook's birthday party

Read the story and tick (✓) the right answers.

> It's Spook's three hundred and first birthday today. Spook is a very friendly ghost and every year he invites everybody to his birthday party. All Spook's friends come, but his sisters, Dolly, Molly and Polly always go out. They can't stand parties, and they don't like Spook's best friend, Nessie.
> The door bell rings. Spook goes to the door and opens it. It's Nessie and she is carrying a big box. "Happy birthday, Spook!" Nessie says. "Are your horrible* sisters here?" "No, no, my friend," Spook says. "They're visiting their German friends Miss Mut and Miss Griff today." "Good," Nessie says. "Here's your present, Spook. I hope you like it."
> "Oh, thank you, Nessie," Spook says. "What is it?"
> "Open it and see."
> Spook opens his present. "Oh," he says. "Wonderful! It's a new head! Oh, thank you very much, Nessie. Now I've got three heads, one with blond hair and two with black hair."
> "Well, I'm sorry it's got black hair," Nessie says. "I know you like green better, but the shop doesn't sell heads with green hair. But do you like your new head's face?"
> "Oh, yes, and I love the eyes – one is red and the other is yellow. And the lovely black tooth! Cool! I can go to school with this head. It's my school head."
> The door bell rings again …
>
> *grauenhaft*

1 Today is Spook's   311th ☐   301st ☐   401st ☐   birthday.

2 Spook has a birthday party   every fifty years ☐   every year ☐   every Saturday ☐.

3 Spook's sisters   enjoy ☐   like ☐   can't stand ☐   parties.

4 The sisters   want to see ☐   don't like ☐   visit ☐   Nessie.

5 Spook's new head has got   black ☐   blond ☐   red ☐   hair.

6 Spook's favourite hair is   black ☐   green ☐   red ☐.

7 Spook's new face has got one red eye and one   brown ☐   green ☐   yellow ☐   eye.

8 Spook wants to use his new head for   eating ☐   sleeping ☐   going to school ☐.

A party

5

3 Speaking: Can you say it in English?

Was sagst du, wenn …

1 … du jemanden zu deiner Geburtstagsfeier einladen möchtest?

   _____

2 … du wissen möchtest, was jemand an seinem Geburtstag machen will?

   _____

3 … du erfahren willst, was das Lieblingsessen von jemandem ist?

   _____

4 … du wissen möchtest, ob jemand Partyspiele mag?

   _____

5 … du sagen möchtest, dass du dich nicht für Modelle interessierst?

   _____

von 10

4 Writing: My birthday

Write six sentences about your birthday in your exercise book. Use these questions.

> When is your birthday?   Is it on or near another birthday in your family?   What do you eat/drink?
>
> Is it always/often/sometimes in school time?   Who do you invite?   What would you like to do?
>
> Who gives you presents?
>
> What do you do on your birthday?   What presents do you get or would you like to get?
>
> Do you have a birthday party?

von 12

5 Grammar: this, that, these, those

Mrs Batson wants to buy a shirt for Charlie. They're in a shop in Camden.
Write *this/these* or *that/those*.

Mrs Batson What about __*those*__ shirts over there, Charlie? They're nice and they're not too expensive.

Charlie What? _____ shirts over there near the door?

Mrs Batson Yes, _____ are the shirts I'm talking about.

Charlie Oh, no. I don't like _____ much. But what about _____ blue shirt here? I like _____ one a lot. It's cool!

Mrs Batson Yes, but just look at _____ prices, Charlie! All _____ shirts here cost too much. We can buy two of _____ shirts over there for the same money!

von 5

Charlie OK, OK, Mum. You're right. Let's forget _____ shirts and go and look at _____ , then.

What I can say 6

1 The sports we like

a) Listen to Jane, Tom and Alex. Tick (✓) the sports you hear.

basketball ☐   tennis ☐   cycling ☐   gymnastics ☐   judo ☐

horse riding ☐   volleyball ☐   table tennis ☐   skating ☐

pony riding ☐   hockey ☐   swimming ☐   football ☐

b) Listen again. What sports do the friends like? Complete the table.

	likes	doesn't like
Alex		
Jane		
Tom		

2 A sports puzzle

Fill in the sports and places.

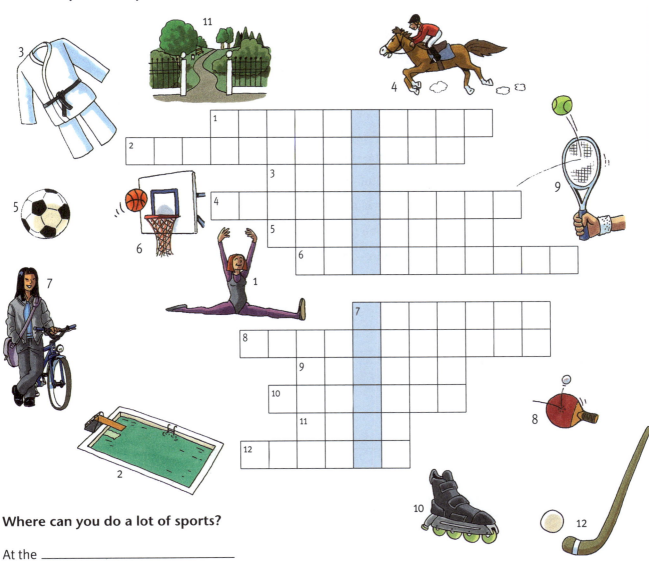

Where can you do a lot of sports?

At the _____

Sports

6

LiF 28R

3 What sports are they doing?

Look at the pictures of sports.
What are the people doing?
Write sentences.

boxing • cycling
doing judo • playing volleyball
swimming • playing tennis
running • playing golf

In the first picture a woman is running.

In the second picture _____

_____

_____

_____

_____

_____

_____

4 Odd one out

a) Circle the odd one out.

1 trainers – football – T-shirt – hat
2 beautiful – wonderful – exciting – boring
3 run – swim – tennis – play
4 nice – bad – great – fantastic
5 nervous – race – sad – excited

b) Now write an odd-one-out puzzle for a partner.

5 Sounds

Say the words and put them in the right list.

easy	close	glasses
price	music	lose
chess	gymnastics	lettuce
cycle	please	trousers
police	cheese	nose

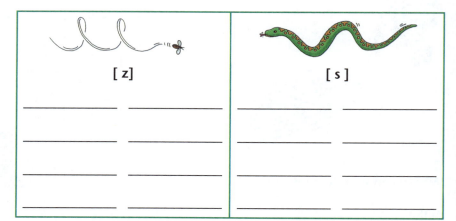

[z]   [s]

6 When? Where? What?

Sports

LiF 8R, 15R

ride play do train write read like …

WHEN DO YOU …?   **WHERE DO YOU …?**   **WHAT DO YOU …?**

make eat go buy watch meet

a) How many questions can you ask?

b) Ask your partner and make notes about his/her answers.

LiF 14R, 16R

c) Now write about your partner. Start like this:

My partner's name is Katrin. She plays darts.

Sports

7 Debbie and the Gunners

Read the dialogue and tick (✓) the correct boxes.

Last Monday it was a sunny day in Regent's Park. Charlie was with Susan and Debbie. Debbie is a big football fan.

Susan There was a game last night. Queen's Park Rangers played against Liverpool. Queen's Park won.
Debbie So what? They're not my favourite team.
Susan OK, OK. What's your favourite team?
Debbie Arsenal, of course. I'm a big fan. They're fantastic.
Charlie You're right, Debbie, but they sometimes lose, too. They lost last Saturday. I saw it on TV.
Debbie Well, you can't always win. But it was a great game and the Gunners were fantastic.
Susan Why do you two like football so much? I think it's boring.
Charlie Oh no, you're wrong, Susan. Football is great. It's really exciting. Do you go to all the Arsenal games, Debbie?
Debbie Well, I usually go to their home games. And every Tuesday and Thursday night I go to the Junior Gunners Club. That's the young fans' club.
Susan What do you do there?
Debbie We often play football, of course, but last Thursday we played darts. We had a competition. I won and got the first prize. It was an Arsenal football shirt.
Charlie Cool! Can I come with you next time?
Debbie Of course, you can, Charlie. What about you, Susan? Do you want to come, too?
Susan Oh, I don't think so, Debbie. Too much football.

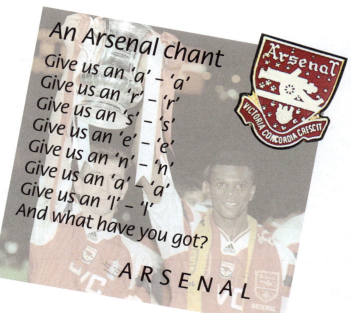

	right	wrong	not in the text
1 There was a football game between Queen's Park Rangers and Arsenal last night.	☐	☐	☐
2 Debbie is a big Queen's Park Rangers fan.	☐	☐	☐
3 Charlie saw the last Arsenal match on TV.	☐	☐	☐
4 Charlie cleaned his football boots last Saturday.	☐	☐	☐
5 Susan thinks football is boring.	☐	☐	☐
6 Charlie agrees with Susan about football.	☐	☐	☐
7 Debbie always goes to Arsenal's home games.	☐	☐	☐
8 Debbie goes to the Junior Gunners Club every Tuesday and Thursday.	☐	☐	☐
9 The Junior Gunners Club is in Victoria Road.	☐	☐	☐
10 Debbie won the darts competition at the Junior Gunners Club last Thursday.	☐	☐	☐
11 Charlie wants to go to the Junior Gunners Club with Debbie.	☐	☐	☐
12 Susan wants to go to the Junior Gunners Club.	☐	☐	☐

8 Do, go, play

a) Fill in the right verb to go with the sport.

do • go • play

YOU
- _____ aerobics
- _____ cycling
- _____ dancing
- _____ football
- _____ gymnastics
- _____ judo
- _____ skating
- _____ swimming
- _____ tennis
- _____ volleyball

b) Can you add the German meanings to these pairs?

win	winner
play	player
ride	rider
drive	driver
run	runner
lose	loser

WORDBANK K sports

9 YOUR club

a) Answer these questions.

Are you a member of a club? _____

What is the name of your club? _____

What does your club do? _____

b) How many clubs are there in your class? Make a list of the clubs on the blackboard.

c) What about a new club? Have you got an idea?
Work with a partner. Make a club card.

PORTFOLIO

How many new members can you find for your club? Ask your classmates.

Sports

6 | 10 And the winner is …

Read A7 in your textbook again. Draw lines.

Flame	turned	the hedge.
Prince and Dark Crystal	crossed	in front of a mouse.
Lionheart	jumped	the finishing line.
Sugar Boy	stopped	round.
Rhonda	fell	Sugar Boy.
Annie	rode	off.
Wally and Paul	won	the race.
Patsy and Flame	left	with no problem.

LiF 22R, 23R, 26R

Sugar Boy told his son about the race. Finish the report.

Do you know what (happen) _____ in the race? When we (begin) _____, we (be) _____ all really fast, but then funny things (start) _____ to happen. First, Lionheart suddenly (stop) _____ because he (see) _____ a mouse! His rider (fall off) _____. Poor Rhonda! She (be) _____ out of the race. And then Dark Crystal and Prince (go) _____ crazy, too. They (jump) _____ the hedge. They (run) _____ across a field and (leave) _____ the race. Now there (be) _____ just two horses in the race, me and Flame. But Flame (be) _____ in front of me and I just (feel) _____ too tired to catch him. So do you know what I (do) _____? I (turn) _____ round, too. So Flame (win) _____ the race.

Flame was the winner of the race. He told the other horses about it. Write his story.

76

11 Odd one out

Circle the odd one out.

1. spent – went – want – slept – kept
2. knew – flew – threw – new – saw
3. walked – fed – cooked – worked – asked
4. tried – helped – lived – cried – bored
5. bought – found – loud – caught – thought
6. felt – kept – market – left – sat

Do you know why 6 is afraid of 7? Because 7, 8, 9.

Computers

6

LiF 26R

12 Where do you get information from?

a) How often do you get information from these things?

	every day	once a week	once a month	never
Internet				
dictionary				
magazines				
TV				
newspapers				
radio				
answering machine				
mobile phone				

 b) Make a class survey about watching TV. First work with a partner. Read the questions and tick (✓) yes/no.

	yes/no		yes/no
1 Have you got a TV in your bedroom?		7 Do you watch TV when you are doing your homework?	
2 Do you watch TV for more than 2 hours a day?		8 Do you watch TV every Saturday morning?	
3 Do you watch the news?		9 Do you watch TV after 10 p.m.?	
4 Do you learn anything from TV?		10 Do you watch TV with your friends?	
5 Do you watch TV in the morning?		11 Do you have a TV-free day?	
6 Do you watch TV when you get home from school?			

c) Collect all your answers in class. Draw a diagram to show the results.

d) Write a report about watching TV in your class.

There are _____ pupils in our class. We talked about watching TV and we made a survey.

These are the results:
- All of us watch …
- Only one pupil …

- Nobody in the class …
- Half the class never watches …
- …

Computers

13 At Ali's computer shop

Listen to a boy and Ali. Tick (✓) the right box.

1. The boy is at Ali's
   a) bookshop ☐
   b) clothes shop ☐
   c) computer shop ☐

2. The boy wants to buy
   a) a mouse ☐
   b) an ink cartridge ☐
   c) an Omex printer ☐

3. The boy's printer is an Omex
   a) 25AP ☐
   b) 25XP ☐
   c) 35AP ☐

4. Colour ink cartidges cost
   a) £26.30 ☐
   b) £26.50 ☐
   c) £24.50 ☐

5. Rajiv can spend
   a) £13 ☐
   b) £30 ☐
   c) £20 ☐

6. Omex really gets its money from
   a) expensive printers ☐
   b) ink cartridges for its printers ☐
   c) mouses ☐

14 Say it in English

Was sagst du auf Englisch, um in einem Geschäft …

1. … den Preis eines Computers zu erfragen?

   _____

2. … jemandem zu sagen, dass du diesen Drucker gern hättest?

   _____

3. … jemanden zu fragen, wie viel etwas kostet?

   _____

4. … jemanden zu fragen, ob er Kopfhörer im Angebot hat?

   _____

5. … jemanden zu fragen, wo sich die DVDs befinden?

   _____

15 Spook's summer job

Spook had a software problem. Correct the mistakes in his email to Nessie.
What is his computer's problem?

Hi Nessie,

Thanks for your postcard from New York. It arrived last month. But I was too busy to send an email. I didn't go on yadiloh _____, I stayed at home and dekrow _____. We needed the money. But I had a great boj _____. I really enjoyed it. Do you know what I did? I took off my daeh _____ and scared the stsiruot _____ in our old castle*. One bad thing was that I got up early to do this – in the elddim _____ of the day! This was because tourists go to deb _____ when I normally get up. Aren't they funny?

I tried hard to scare the tourists, but I wasn't very doog _____ at it. They weren't really frightened of me – a lot of them just dehgual _____. "Look at that silly tsohg _____," they said. I was too friendly, that was the problem. My boss said, "Spook, you ot evah _____ stop this. I don't want you to say to people, 'Hi, everybody. Don't worry. It's only old koopS _____.'"

Boo ;-) from

Your friend Spook   Boo! ;-)

*Burg

16 Charlie's school magazine

Charlie is interviewing you for the school magazine. Put in the short answers for YOU.

- Have you got a computer at home? — Yes, I have. / No, I haven't.
- Are you sometimes late for school? — Yes, I am. / No, I'm not.
- Do you surf the Internet? — Yes, I do. / No, I don't.
- Did you meet your friends yesterday? — Yes, I did. / No, I didn't.

1 Have you got a pet? _____
2 Do you watch lots of TV? _____
3 Does your mother work? _____
4 Are you in a club? _____
5 Can you speak English? _____
6 Is your best friend at your school? _____
7 Have you got any brothers or sisters? _____
8 Did you enjoy your last birthday? _____
9 Did you go on holiday last year? _____
10 Can you play tennis? _____

Computers

17 Free time activities

 Match the questions with the right answers.

1 Isn't this a great club?
2 Are there club meetings every week?
3 Can we get refreshments here?
4 Have they got club T-shirts?
5 Do you always go to the meetings?
6 Can I come next time, too?

(s) Yes, of course you can come.
(s) Yes, it is.
(r) No, they haven't, but you can get club stickers.
(o) Yes, the cafeteria is over there.
(t) Yes, I do.
(p) Yes, we meet every Tuesday and Thursday.

Write the letters here and find out what kind of club it is.

1	2	3	4	5	6

Now write the dialogue in your exercise book.

Write the other part of this dialogue.

Andrew

YOU

1 Hello _____! _____

2 Let's go skating today.   _____

3 Do you like old cars?   _____

4 Let's go to the car museum!   _____

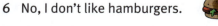 _____

5 Yes, I'm hungry, too. _____

6 No, I don't like hamburgers.   _____

7 Well, pizza is a good idea. _____

 Write an activity report in your exercise book. Say what you do and where you go after school. What have you got for your activity?

18 Weather report

Listen to the CD and tick (✓).

CD

TIP
Look at the map at the back of your textbook.

	windy	rainy	cloudy	snowy	foggy	sunny
Scotland	☐	☐	☐	☐	☐	☐
North of England	☐	☐	☐	☐	☐	☐
South of England	☐	☐	☐	☐	☐	☐
Wales	☐	☐	☐	☐	☐	☐
Ireland	☐	☐	☐	☐	☐	☐
Northern Ireland	☐	☐	☐	☐	☐	☐

snowy – *schneereich*
foggy – *neblig*

19 Weather poems

Write your poem.

rain
rainy day
long rainy day
very long rainy day
– games

summer holidays
fun with my friends
cool lemonade
cycling
happy people

PORTFOLIO

Computers

6

20 **The Camden Market game**

You need:

Play this game in a group of 2–5 people.
When you come to a person answer the question.

Correct answer: Move 3 circles +
Wrong answer: Move 2 circles –

Who went to Brighton on holiday?

Where is Caroline from?

What pets have the Camden Market children got?

Name five school subjects.

Are the Yorkshire Moors in the north or south of England?

What presents did David get for his birthday?

Test yourself

Bearbeite die *Test yourself*-Seiten wie in den letzten *Themes*. Fülle anschließend den Portfolio-Fragebogen für *Theme* 6 aus. Außerdem gibt es in deinem Portfolio-Heft noch einen Fragenbogen, mit dem du herausfinden kannst, welche Lerntechniken dir am besten beim Lernen helfen.

1 Listening: In a clothes shop

Listen and tick (✓) the right box.   RIGHT   WRONG

1 The first jeans cost £30.
2 The boy says the first jeans are too expensive.
3 The second jeans are green.
4 The second jeans cost £20.
5 The boy tries the jeans on behind a door.
6 The first jeans the boy tries on are too small.
7 The second jeans the boy tries on are too big.
8 The boy gets £2 change.

von 16

2 Grammar: Present progressive

Look at the four pictures. Say what is happening.

Charlie is the commentator. He ___is telling___ everybody what ___is happening___. The five riders ___are___ on their ponies. They _____ for the race to start. **(sit, happen, wait, tell)**

Lionheart _____ suddenly because of a mouse and Rhonda _____ through the air. Three people _____ Lionheart and Rhonda. **(stop, watch, fly)**

Two ponies _____ the race. They _____ over a hedge. A boy _____ out of the picture. **(jump, run, leave)**

Patsy and Flame _____ the finishing line. Charlie and the other people _____ and they _____ "Well done, Patsy!"

(cross, shout, laugh)

von 5,5

Free time

3 Reading: Cybercamp

Read the text and tick (✔) the right answer.

> Hi. My name's Ken Marks from New York. I go to a summer camp every year. It's my best holiday. There are summer camps in America for just about everything. There are camps for different sports, camps for music and even* camps for learning to drive. I always go to a 'cybercamp' outside Boston. Last year, I went there for three weeks in August. I had a wonderful time.
> There were 20 kids in my group and they all knew <u>a lot</u> about computers! We had lessons in the morning and the teachers showed us how to write computer programs. That was cool.
> In the afternoon, we did other things. We went swimming, played basketball or went to interesting places around Boston.
> We had a lot of fun in the evening too. They often let us have new software games to test for hours. Or we just sat outside and talked – I made lots of new friends.

*sogar

1 Ken … goes to summer camp.
   a) often ☐
   b) never ☐
   c) always ☐

2 Summer camps usually teach you
   a) one thing. ☐
   b) many different things. ☐
   c) sports, music and driving. ☐

3 Ken's summer camp was
   a) in New York. ☐
   b) near Boston. ☐
   c) in the centre of Boston. ☐

4 Ken's group was for kids who
   a) wanted a wonderful time. ☐
   b) were very good with computers. ☐
   c) knew how to write computer programs. ☐

5 They learned about computers
   a) all day. ☐
   b) in the morning. ☐
   c) morning and afternoon. ☐

6 The evening was fun because they
   a) wrote new software. ☐
   b) went to interesting places. ☐
   c) made new friends. ☐

4 Writing: A postcard home

You are at cybercamp with Ken. Write a postcard home. Say what you do during the day and the evening and if you are enjoying yourself.

LiF in short

1 Can/can't

- Mit dem Modalverb **can** sagst du, was du tun kannst, mit **can't,** was du nicht tun kannst oder darfst.
- **Can** ist bei allen Personen gleich. Fragen und Antworten werden immer mit der selben Form gebildet.

> *You can have an ice cream but you can't have an apple.*
> *Can I have this T-shirt? – No, you can't.*

2 There is/there are

- Wenn eine Sache oder eine Person vorhanden ist, sagst du **there is,** bei mehreren Sachen oder Personen **there are.**

> *There is a sandwich shop in the street.*
> *There are five bus stops in the street.*

3 Mehrzahl

- Die Mehrzahl von Nomen bildest du meist, indem du ein **-s** an das Wort anhängst:
  *1 earring – 2 earring**s***
- Wörter, die mit einem Zischlaut enden, erhalten in der Mehrzahl ein **-es:**
  *1 glass – 5 glass**es**   1 sandwich – 2 sandwich**es***
- **-y** wird zu **-ies** nach einem Konsonant:
  *hobby – hobb**ies.***
- Es gibt Wörter, die nur die Einzahl oder nur die Mehrzahl bilden:
  food, homework (nur Einzahl)
  jeans, clothes (nur Einzahl)
- Es gibt Wörter, die die Mehrzahl nicht mit **-s** bilden:
  1 man – 2 men   1 foot – 8 feet

4 Have got

Langform	Kurzform	
I have got	I've got	*ich habe*
you have got	you've got	*du hast, Sie haben*
he has got	he's got	*er hat*
she has got	she's got	*sie hat*
it has got	it's got	*es hat*
we have got	we've got	*wir haben*
you have got	you've got	*ihr habt, Sie haben*
they have got	they've got	*sie haben*

- Um zu sagen, was du nicht hast, stellst du **not** zwischen **have/has** und got.

Langform	Kurzform
I have not got a dog.	I haven't got a dog.
She has not got a brother.	She hasn't got a brother.

- Um eine Frage zu bilden, tauschst du **have/has** und das Personalpronomen.
  She (1) has (2) got a cat. → Has (2) she (1) got a cat?
- Kurzantwort: Es klingt etwas unhöflich, wenn du nur **yes** or **no** auf eine Frage antwortest. Deshalb fügst du eine Kurzantwort an.

Frage	+	−
Have you got a sister?	Yes, I have.	No, I haven't.
Has Charlie got a pen?	Yes, he has.	No, he hasn't.

5 Der Artikel

- Es gibt nur eine Form des bestimmten Artikels: **the** (der, die, das).
- Der unbestimmte Artikel (ein/eine) heißt **a** oder **an.** Vor Vokalen steht **an.**
  a book aber an apple

6 Personalpronomen

I	*ich*
you	*du/Sie*
he	*er*
she	*sie*
it	*es*
we	*wir*
you	*ihr/Sie*
they	*sie*

 he

 she

 it

- **I** wird immer groß geschrieben, auch wenn es mitten im Satz vorkommt.
- **you** kann sowohl „du" als auch „Sie" oder „ihr" heißen.

LiF in short

7 Das Verb „be"

- Beim Sprechen benutzt du die Kurzform von **be**, beim Schreiben oft die Langform.

Langform	Kurzform	
I am	I'm	ich bin
you are	you're	du bist, Sie sind
he is	he's	er ist
she is	she's	sie ist
it is	it's	es ist
we are	we're	wir sind
you are	you're	ihr seid, Sie sind
they are	they're	sie sind

- Die Kurzform von **is** wird häufig nach anderen Wörtern benutzt:
where's, what's, who's, there's, that's.

8 Fragen mit Fragewörtern

- Um zu erfahren was, wann, wo und warum etwas passiert, stellst du Bestimmungsfragen mit den Fragewörtern.
What is your name?
When can you come?

what	was?
when	wann?
where	wo?
who	wer?
whose	wessen?
why	warum?

9 Verneinung von „be"

- Wenn du das Verb **be** in der Verneinung benutzt, wird an die entsprechende Form **not** angehängt.

Langform	Kurzform	
I am not	I'm not	ich bin nicht
you are not	you aren't	du bist nicht, Sie sind nicht
he is not	he isn't	er ist nicht
she is not	she isn't	sie ist nicht
it is not	it isn't	es ist nicht
we are not	we aren't	wir sind nicht
you are not	you aren't	ihr seid nicht, Sie sind nicht
they are not	they aren't	sie sind nicht

10 Fragen und Kurzantworten

- Im Englischen fügst du bei Fragen, die man mit ja oder nein beantworten kann, eine zusätzliche Bestätigung oder Ablehnung hinzu.

Frage	+	–
Is Caroline from Manchester?	Yes, she is.	No, she isn't.
Are we all ready?	Yes, we are.	No, we aren't.

11 Possessivpronomen

- Mit Possessivpronomen kannst du sagen, wem etwas oder zu wem jemand gehört.
- **Its** benutzt du bei Dingen und Tieren.
*The dog is in **its** house.*

my	mein/e
your	dein/e, Ihr/e
his	sein/e
her	ihr/e
its	sein/e
our	unser/e
your	euer/eure, Ihr/e
their	ihr/e

12 Der Imperativ

- Der Imperativ hat im Englischen immer dieselbe Form, egal ob du eine oder mehrere Personen ansprichst.
Wash your face!
Open your books!
- Bei der Verneinung stellst du **don't** vor das Verb im Infinitiv.
Don't forget your books!

13 Präpositionen

- Um zu sagen, wo sich etwas befindet, benutzt du Präpositionen: **in** (on), **on** (auf), **in front of** (vor), **behind** (hinter), **next to** (neben), **under** (unter).

14 Die einfache Gegenwart (simple present)

- Das **simple present** benutzt du, wenn du über Gewohnheiten oder regelmäßige Ereignisse sprichst. Du benutzt es auch, wenn du beschreibst, dass jemand mehrere Dinge nacheinander tut (z. B. in einer Geschichte).
- Das **simple present** hat dieselbe Form wie der Infinitiv. Nur bei **he, she** und **it** wird ein **-s** angehängt.

simple present		
I	learn	English.
You	learn	maths.
He	learn**s**	German.
She	learn**s**	music.
It	learn**s**	tricks.
We	learn	sport.
You	learn	songs.
They	learn	games.

- Endet das Verb mit einem Zischlaut, muss bei **he, she, it** ein **-es** angehängt werden.
You wash your face.
*He wash**es** his face.*
- Einige Verben haben eine besondere Schreibweise.
I do my homework.   *They tidy their room.*
*He do**es** his homework.*   *He tid**ies** his room.*

LiF in short

15 Die einfache Gegenwart: Fragen und Kurzantworten

- Fragen, die du mit **yes** oder **no** beantwortest, werden mit **do/does** gebildet.

Frage	+	–
Do you know her?	Yes, I do.	No, I don't.
Does Caroline tidy her room?	Yes, she does.	No, she doesn't.

- Die Fragewörter stehen immer am Anfang.
 What do you eat for breakfast?
 Where does Charlie eat breakfast?

16 Die einfache Gegenwart: Verneinung

- Du verneinst Sätze in der Gegenwart mit **don't**. Bei **he, she, it** benutzt man **doesn't**.

simple present		
I	don't	learn English.
You	don't	learn maths.
He	doesn't	learn German.
She	doesn't	learn music.
It	doesn't	learn tricks.
We	don't	learn sport.
You	don't	learn songs.
They	don't	learn games.

17 Häufigkeitsadverbien

- Wenn du sagen willst, wie oft du etwas machst, benutzt du Häufigkeitsadverbien. Diese Wörter stehen meistens zwischen Subjekt und Verb.

Subjekt	Adverb	Verb	Objekt		
wer	wie oft	tut	was	(mit wem, wo, wann, usw.)	
I	always	play	football	with my friends.	immer
Hoover	usually	has	a bath	on Fridays.	normalerweise
Gillian	sometimes	helps	her brother	with his homework.	manchmal
Charlie	often	takes	his sister	to ballet school.	oft
They	never	come	late	to school	nie

18 s-Genitiv

- Um zu sagen, wem oder zu wem etwas/jemand gehört, hängst du im Englischen ein Apostroph und ein **s ('s)** an den/die „Besitzer/in" an.
 Rajiv's maths teacher.
 Gillian's cat.

19 Personalpronomen als Objekt

- Im Deutschen fragst du nach dieser Form von Personalpronomen mit *wem* oder *wen*.
 Im Englischen gibt es nur eine Objektform:
 Gillian can help **him**. *Gillian kann ihm helfen. (wem?)*
 Gillian can see **him**. *Gillian kann ihn sehen. (wen?)*

Subjekt	Objekt	
I	me	mir, mich
you	you	dir, dich; Ihnen, Sie
he	him	ihm, ihn
she	her	ihr, sie
it	it	ihm, ihn/es
we	us	uns, uns
you	you	euch; Ihnen, Sie
they	them	ihnen, sie

20 Must/have to

- Mit dem Modalhilfsverb **must** sagst du, was du tun musst.
 I must go to bed at 10 o'clock.
- Du kannst **must** mit **have to** ersetzen. Es bedeutet dasselbe.
 Gillian has to do her homework before she can go out.
- Wenn du sagen willst, dass jemand etwas nicht zu tun braucht, benutzt du **don't have to.**
 You don't have to help me with my homework. It's easy.

21 Wortstellung

- Der Bauplan einfacher englischer Sätze sieht meist so aus:

Subjekt	Verb	Objekt	
wer	tut	was	(mit wem, wo, wann, usw.)
I	play	football	with my friends. in the park. in the afternoon.

LiF in short

22 Die Vergangenheit von „be"

- Das **simple past** wird verwendet, wenn du über etwas sprechen willst, das in der Vergangenheit stattgefunden hat – gestern, letzte Woche, letztes Jahr.
- Die Vergangenheit von **be** hat zwei Formen: **was** und **were**.
- In Fragen mit **was/were** stellst du **was** oder **were** an den Satzanfang.
  Was the room cold and wet?
  – Yes, it was.
  Were they afraid?
  – No, they weren't.

simple past: be	
I	was
you	were
he	was
she	was
it	was
we	were
you	were
they	were

- Für die Verneinung hängst du **not** oder die Kurzform **-n't** an **was/were** an.
  The room wasn't cold and wet.

23 Die einfache Vergangenheit (simple past): regelmäßige Verben

- In der einfachen Vergangenheit gibt es bei regelmäßigen Verben nur eine Verbform für alle Personen: du hängst die Endung **-ed** an den Infinitiv an.
  I play with the cat → I played with the cat.
- Bei Verben, die im Infinitiv auf **-e** enden, wird nur **-d** angehängt: *love → loved.*

24 Die einfache Vergangenheit: Fragen und Kurzantworten

- Ja/nein-Fragen bildest du, indem du **did** an den Satzanfang stellst.
  Did you go on holiday? Yes, we did.
  Did Jack like the farm? No, he didn't.
- **Did** wird bei allen Personen verwendet.
- **Did** zeigt bereits die Vergangenheit an. Deshalb lässt du das Verb im Infinitiv.
- Bei Fragen mit Fragewort steht zuerst das Fragewort, dann folgt **did** oder **was/were**.
  Where did you go on holiday?
  What did you do?

25 Die einfache Vergangenheit: Verneinung

- Wenn du sagen willst, was in der Vergangenheit nicht geschehen ist, musst du **didn't** vor das Verb stellen. Das Verb bleibt im Infinitiv, weil **didn't** schon die Vergangenheit anzeigt.
- Die Form **didn't** ist bei allen Personen gleich.
  She didn't go away for her holidays.
  They didn't play football yesterday.

26 Die einfache Vergangenheit: unregelmäßige Verben

- Viele Verben bilden die Vergangenheitsform nicht mit **-ed**. Sie sind unregelmäßig.
- Die Vergangenheitsform von **have** ist **had** und die von **do** ist **did**. Die Formen sind für alle Personen gleich.
- Weitere unregelmäßige Verben findest du in diesen Sätzen:
  Emma went to the Yorkshire Moors.
  She saw a lot of sheep.
  She fell in a bog.
- Eine Liste der unregelmäßigen Verben findest du auf der letzten Seite dieses Buches.

27 This/that – these/those

- **This** und **that** benutzt du, wenn du zwei Sachen oder Personen unterscheiden willst.
- **This** benutzt du für etwas, das in der Nähe des Sprechers/der Sprecherin ist;
  that wird verwendet für etwas, das weiter weg ist.
- Bei mehreren Sachen oder Personen benutzt du **these** und **those**.

28 Die Verlaufsform (present progressive)

- Wenn du sagen möchtest, was gerade passiert oder was du gerade tust, benutzt du das **present progressive**.
- Sie wird mit einer Form von **be** (**am, is, are**) und der **-ing** Form des Verbs gebildet.

I	am	listen**ing** to music.
You	are	stand**ing** on my foot.
It	is	rain**ing**.
We	are	watch**ing** TV.

- Endet das Verb auf **-e**, fällt das **-e** weg:

  make → making

- Bei einigen Verben wird der letzte Buchstabe verdoppelt:

  sit → sitting
  swim → swimming

29 Die Verlaufsform: Fragen und Verneinung

- Bei Fragen tauschst du einfach das Subjekt und die Form von **be**.

Frage	+	–
Is Charlie helping his dad?	Yes, he is.	No, he isn't.
Are they doing a card trick?	Yes, they are.	No, they aren't.

- Bei der Verneinung fügst du einfach **not** zur Form von **be** hinzu.
  Rajiv isn't reading a book. He's cleaning the kitchen.

Test yourself – Lösungen

Diese Lösungsseiten findest du auch im Internet unter:
www.diesterweg.de/camden-market/download

Hier findest du die Lösungen zu Test yourself. Vergleiche sie mit deinen Antworten. Natürlich kannst du zusätzlich mit einem Partner oder einer Partnerin vergleichen, wie ihr die Aufgaben bearbeitet habt. Trage deine Punktzahl ein, nachdem du jede Aufgabe überprüft hast, und addiere abschließend deine Punkte. Unten auf der Seite findest du eine Gesamtbewertung und wichtige Lerntipps.

Listening: New friends

1 What's **your** name?
2 **I'm** from Manchester.
3 Welcome to **Camden**.
4 I've got a collection of **CDs**.
5 **Her** name is Butterfly.
6 I love **ice cream**.

Für jede richtige Lösung erhältst du zwei Punkte.

Meine Punkte: ☐ von 12

Speaking: Can you say it in English?

1	2	3	4	5	6
F	R	I	E	N	D

Für jede richtige Zuordnung erhältst du einen halben Punkt.

Meine Punkte: ☐ von 3

Words: Odd one out

1 dog
2 red
3 nice
4 dirty
5 game
6 camera

Für jede richtige Lösung erhältst du einen halben Punkt.

Meine Punkte: ☐ von 3

Reading: Charlie Batson

1 true
2 true
3 not in the text
4 false
5 false
6 true
7 not in the text
8 false

Für jede richtige Lösung erhältst du zwei Punkte.

Meine Punkte: ☐ von 16

Writing: An email

Mögliche Lösung:
Hi ...,
My name is <u>Lisa</u> and I live <u>in Eberswalde</u>.
I go <u>to the Bruno-H.-Bürgel</u> School. I'm <u>in</u> class <u>5a</u> there.
My hair <u>is black</u> and my eyes <u>are brown</u>.
My favourite colour <u>is red</u>, my favourite animal <u>is a dog</u>
and my favourite sport <u>is football</u>. Are you <u>interested in sport</u>?
What <u>is your favourite hobby</u>?
Goodbye, <u>Lisa</u>

Für jede richtige Lösung erhältst du zwei Punkte.

Meine Punkte: ☐ von 10

Auswertung:

40–48 Punkte: Super! Du kannst schon sehr viel auf Englisch sagen und schreiben. Mach weiter so!

32–39 Punkte: Du weißt bereits eine ganze Menge, das ist toll! Sieh dir die Aufgaben aber trotzdem noch einmal genau an. Wo hast du Fehler gemacht? Lies dann unten die entsprechenden Tipps.

31 Punkte und weniger: Du solltest das *Theme* noch einmal gut einsehen. Nur Mut! Wenn du dich jetzt nochmal intensiv damit befasst, holst du leicht auf. Sieh dir auch die fünf Aufgaben dieser Seite nochmal an. Welche sind dir schwer gefallen? Die folgenden Tipps helfen dir beim Wiederholen und Üben.

Meine Punkte insgesamt: ☐ von 48

Lerntipps:

- **Listening:** Falls dir die Höraufgabe schwer gefallen ist, höre dir möglichst häufig englische Kassetten oder CDs an. Lies auch die Hinweise *How to listen* auf Seite 129 im Textbook.
- **Speaking:** Auf Seite 4 im Workbook findest du in Aufgabe 8 wichtige Redewendungen, die du lernen solltest.
- **Words:** Wie man sich Wörter gut merkt, erfährst du im Textbook auf Seite 130 und 131.
- **Reading:** Hier war gefragt, sorgfältig zu lesen und Details herauszufinden. Falls du Fehler gemacht hast, überlege, ob du dich gründlich genug mit dem Text befasst oder manche Wörter vielleicht nicht verstanden hast.
- **Writing:** Hattest du hier Probleme, dann befasse dich noch einmal intensiv damit, wie man Auskunft über sich und andere erteilt. In *Theme* 1 gibt es mehrere Texte und Aufgaben dazu.

Test yourself – Lösungen

Hier findest du wieder die Lösungen und die Auswertung zu *Test yourself*. Überprüfe, ob deine Antworten richtig sind. Errechne die Punktzahl, die du bei jeder Aufgabe erzielt hast, und zähle abschließend alle Punkte zusammen. Lies dann die Auswertung und beachte die nützlichen Lerntipps.

1 Listening: Emma and Jack

1 *true*   3 *false*   5 *true*   7 *true*
2 *false* 4 *true*   6 *true*   8 *false*

Für jede richtige Lösung erhältst du zwei Punkte.

Meine Punkte: von 16

2 Reading: Camden Dog School

1 *school*   3 *break*   5 *boring*
2 *half past nine* 4 *likes* 6 *right*

Für jede richtige Lösung erhältst du zwei Punkte.

Meine Punkte: von 12

3 Words: Time words

t–o–d–a–y
t–o–m–o–r–r–o–w
d–a–y
w–e–e–k
m–o–n–t–h
y–e–a–r

Für jede richtige Lösung erhältst du einen halben Punkt.

Meine Punkte: von 3

4 Speaking: Say it in English, please.

1 *What time is it, please?*
2 *Sorry, could you say that again, please?*
3 *(Excuse me,) Could I have a pencil, please?*
4 *Do/Would you mind if I open the window?*
5 *What is 'bin' in German, please?*

Für jeden richtigen Satz erhältst du 2 Punkte. Manchmal gibt es mehrere Möglichkeiten. Frag deinen Lehrer oder deine Lehrerin, wenn du dir nicht sicher bist.

Meine Punkte: von 10

5 Writing: Your favourite school day

a) Wie die Schulfächer auf Englisch heißen, steht auf Seite 38 und 140 im Textbook.
b) Mögliche Antworten:
1 *My favourite day is Monday because I have got only five lessons.*
2 *My first lesson <u>starts</u> at 8 o'clock./<u>finishes</u> at 8.45 a.m.*
3 *My second lesson is sports. I like it because I'm good at it.*
4 *My favourite lesson <u>starts</u> at 10.30. It is my favourite because the teacher is great.*

In a) erhältst du für den Wochentag und jedes richtig geschriebene Schulfach einen halben Punkt.

Meine Punkte: von 3,5

In b) erhältst du für Nr. 1–3 jeweils zwei Punkte, für Nr. 4 vier Punkte.

Meine Punkte: von 10

6 Grammar: Simple present

1 *loves*   2 *dance*   3 *gets*   4 *go*   5 *finishes*

Für jede richtige Verbform erhältst du einen halben Punkt.

Meine Punkte: von 2,5

Auswertung:

Meine Punkte insgesamt: von 57

48–57 Punkte: Wirklich klasse! Du hast schon eine ganze Menge gelernt. Bleib am Ball!
29–37 Punkte: Gar nicht schlecht, aber du hast bestimmt gemerkt, dass du in manchen Bereichen noch nicht ganz fit bist. Überlege, wo du dich unsicher fühlst. Lies die Tipps und hole nach, was noch nicht richtig sitzt.
28 Punkte und weniger: Nicht verzagen! Überprüfe erst einmal, bei welchen Aufgaben du nur wenige Punkte bekommen hast. Befolge dann die Tipps. Tu dies lieber heute als morgen!

Lerntipps
- **Listening:** Je öfter du dir englische Texte anhörst, umso besser wirst du Einzelheiten verstehen. Oder wie wäre es mit englischem Fernsehen, zum Beispiel mit Musiksendungen?
- **Reading:** Hast du hier Fehler gemacht, dann arbeite den Text noch einmal gründlich durch, bis du das Gefühl hast, wirklich alle wichtigen Informationen verstanden zu haben.
- **Words:** Versuche, dir neue Wörter mit Wortbildern einzuprägen. Wie das geht, steht im Textbook auf Seite 165.
- **Speaking:** Präge dir die Redewendungen auf Seite 17 im Workbook ein (Aufgabe 6, *Say it in English*).
- **Writing:** Wenn du Schwierigkeiten hattest, weil dir die Wörter rund um das Thema Schule nicht eingefallen sind, wiederhole die entsprechenden Aufgaben im Textbook und im Workbook. Lege eine Wordbank an.
- **Grammar:** Bist du schon mit dem *LiF*-Teil vertraut? Darin wird die Grammatik mit vielen Beispielen erklärt.

Test yourself – Lösungen

Nun bist du schon vertraut mit den Test-yourself-Aufgaben. Vergleiche deine Antworten wieder mit den Lösungen und addiere deine Punkte. Die Auswertung und Lerntipps findest du unten auf der Seite.

Listening: Kenny's room

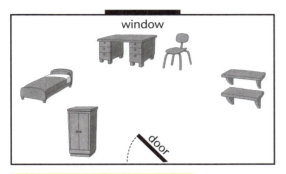

Für jedes richtig angeordnete Möbelstück erhältst du zwei Punkte.

Meine Punkte: von 10

2 Reading: Tom's dream room

*My dream room has a **basketball basket** so that I can play **basketball** every day. It is a big room. There are **blue elephants** on the wall – my favourite animals. There is a shelf for my **elephants**, too. **I've got** a desk. I keep my pens and pencils **on my desk**. I have got a poster with my favourite **football player** on it. He has got a **red T-shirt** and **red** hair. I have got a new **CD player** so I can listen to rap music. I love hip hop! I **can**'t watch TV in my room.*

Für jeden verbesserten Fehler erhältst du einen Punkt.

Meine Punkte: von 10

Speaking: Giving directions

Go straight on. Turn right into Kentish Town Road. At the end of Kentish Town Road turn left into Parkway and keep straight. Go across the canal. Turn into the second street on the left after the canal. That's Ryl College Street. The station is on your left.

Für jede Richtungsanweisung erhältst du zwei Punkte.

Meine Punkte: von 10

4 Writing: My room

Hi, my (new) room is great. My desk is under the window. I keep my books, pens and pencils on my desk. My bed is opposite the window, next to my wardrobe. My CD player is next to my bed. I often listen to music in my room. There is a big shelf for books in my room, too. What's your room like? CU, Nico

Du solltest mindestens vier Sätze geschrieben haben. Für jeden Satz erhältst du einen Punkt.

Meine Punkte: von 8

Grammar: An interview

1 *Do you live with your parents?/with your dad?*
2 *Do you eat meat?*
3 *Does your cat like dogs?*
4 *Do you make your own bed?*
5 *Does your grandma forget things?*

Für jede richtige Frage erhältst du einen halben Punkt.

Meine Punkte: von 2,5

Meine Punkte insgesamt: von 40,5

Auswertung:
33–40,5 Punkte: Super! Du kommst mühelos mit unterschiedlichen Aufgabenstellungen klar.
27–32 Punkte: Eine ordentliche Leistung. Untersuche trotzdem nochmal genau, wo du Fehler gemacht hast. Befasse dich dann mit den Tipps und übe das, was notwendig ist.
26 Punkte und weniger: Die Inhalte dieses *Theme* bereiten dir noch Schwierigkeiten. Halte dir zwei Nachmittage oder ein Wochenende frei und arbeite es gründlich nach. Lies die Tipps und nutze sie bei der Wiederholung.

Lerntipps
- **Listening:** Es ist wichtig, dass du dich vor Höraufgaben entspannst. Schließe die Augen und achte nur auf das, was dir vorgespielt wird. Wenn du jemanden kennst, der gut Englisch spricht, dann bitte ihn, dir öfter mal etwas vorzulesen. Auch dadurch schulst du dein Gehör.
- **Reading:** Achte beim Lesen darauf, welcher Leseauftrag dir gestellt wird. Es ist ein Unterschied, ob du alles wiedergeben oder aber nur bestimmte Informationen herausfiltern sollst. Letzteres war hier gefordert.
- **Speaking:** Wenn du bei der Wegbeschreibung unsicher warst, siehe dir noch einmal Seite 58 und 59 im Textbook und Seite 38 im Workbook an.
- **Writing:** Das freie Schreiben fällt dir noch schwer? Mache dir keinen Stress, sondern übe einfach Schritt für Schritt. Fange damit an, dass du kleine Texte abschreibst. So bekommst du ein Gefühl dafür, wie englische Sätze aufgebaut sind. Das Formulieren gelingt dann mit der Zeit immer besser.
- **Grammar:** Sprich noch einmal mit einem Partner/einer Partnerin über die neue Grammatik in diesem Theme. Lest gemeinsam den *LiF*-Teil und geht Aufgabe 5 nochmal durch. Fragen stellen kann man gut zu zweit üben.

Test yourself – Lösungen

Vergleiche deine Antworten mit den folgenden Lösungen und zähle deine Punkte zusammen.

1 Listening: Our pets

1 *snake* 2 *dog* 3 *cat* 4 *parrot* 5 *rabbit*

Für jedes richtige Tier erhältst du zwei Punkte.

Meine Punkte: ☐ von 10

2 Reading: Penguins or elephants?

		Penguins	Elephants
1	Where do they come from?	all over the world	Africa and Asia
2	What do they eat?	fish	hay (drink water)
3	What do they do?	good swimmers; have a funny walk	work hard
4	What do the keepers do?	feed the penguins fish	take elephants for long walks; sit on their backs

Für jeden Eintrag erhältst du einen Punkt.

Meine Punkte: ☐ von 10

3 Words: Odd one out

1 *milk* 2 *swim* 3 *arrive* 4 *rain* 5 *fast* 6 *shout*

Für jede richtige Lösung erhältst du einen halben Punkt.

Meine Punkte: ☐ von 3

4 Speaking: What do these sentences tell you?

They eat snails and drink water. **A**   It has got beautiful soft fur. **A**
Clean her cage every week. **C**   He ran away from the zoo. **B**
Don't give her milk. **C**
Then he swam in the canal and walked in the park. **B**

Für jede richtige Zuordnung erhältst du einen Punkt.

Meine Punkte: ☐ von 6

5 Writing: Emma's postcard

Mögliche Lösung: Hi Caroline,
We are here for two weeks. The moors are beautiful, but the nearest shops are five miles away! The farm animals are unfriendly and don't like strangers. A stupid thing happened yesterday. We went for a walk and suddenly we were in a bog up to our knees! We couldn't move! But Grandma found us. She took a funny photo! Her two ponies Mumbo and Jumbo helped us out. I want to be home in Camden soon!! Emma

Für jeden Satz, den du geschrieben hast, erhältst du zwei Punkte. (Wenn du dir nicht sicher bist, wie viele Punkte du dir geben sollst, besprich dich mit einem Partner/einer Partnerin.)

Meine Punkte: ☐ von 12

6 Grammar: Simple past

came; lived; was; was; had; ran; caught; went; swam; felt; slept; played; talked

Für jede richtige Verbform erhältst du einen halben Punkt.

Meine Punkte: ☐ von 6,5

Auswertung:

40–47,5 Punkte: Klasse, du wirst immer besser. Bleib so gut!
31–39 Punkte: Bei dir ist eine ganze Menge des neuen Stoffs hängen geblieben. Wo warst du noch unsicher? Lies die Tipps und befasse dich noch einmal mit den Aspekten, die dir Schwierigkeiten bereitet haben.
30 Punkte und weniger: Das genügt leider noch nicht. Fühle dich bitte durch diese Aussage nicht kritisiert, sondern lies in Ruhe die Tipps und nimm dir dann ausreichend Zeit, das *Theme* noch einmal zu wiederholen.

Meine Punkte insgesamt: ☐ von 47,5

Lerntipps:

- **Listening:** Bei Höraufgaben geht es meist nicht darum, jedes Wort zu verstehen. Es ist wichtig, Schlüsselwörter herauszuhören. Wenn es um *pets* geht, ist *loves mice* z. B. der „Schlüssel", dass es um eine Katze geht.
- **Reading:** Hier ging es um das genaue Lesen. Dazu musst du einen Text mindestens zweimal, vielleicht auch öfter lesen. Übe das, indem du öfter unbekannte Texte liest. Wie wäre es mit *Reading is fun* hinten im Textbook?
- **Words:** Fällt dir Vokabellernen schwer? Dann geh einmal den *Words*-Teil im Textbook durch. Da werden Methoden erklärt, wie du dir Wortschatz einprägen kannst. Zwei oder drei davon helfen dir bestimmt.
- **Speaking:** Die Sätze stammen aus dem Textbook. Blättere noch einmal das *Theme* durch, bis du sie findest.
- **Writing:** Nimm dir nach dem Schreiben immer ausreichend Zeit für das Korrekturlesen!
- **Grammar:** Falls du hier Schwierigkeiten hattest, schreibe dir die unregelmäßigen Verben (ganz hinten im Workbook) zum Lernen auf Wortkarten. Die unregelmäßigen Verben brauchst du ständig. Deshalb müssen sie sitzen.

Test yourself – Lösungen

Hier sind die Lösungen zu *Test yourself*. Vergleiche sie mit deinen Antworten und errechne deine Punktzahl pro Aufgabe sowie deine Gesamtpunktzahl. Lies dann die Auswertung und die Lerntipps unten auf der Seite.

1 Listening: Dates

14th February; 30th April; 15th April
21st May; 8th February; 22nd June

Für jedes richtig abgehakte Datum erhältst du zwei Punkte.

Meine Punkte: ☐ von 12

2 Reading: Spook's birthday party

1 Today is Spook's **301st** birthday.
2 Spook has a birthday party **every year**.
3 Spook's sisters **can't stand** parties.
4 The sisters **don't like** Nessie.
5 Spook's new head has got **black** hair.
6 Spook's favourite hair is **green**.
7 Spook's new face has got one red eye and one **yellow** eye.
8 Spook wants to use his new head for **going to school**.

Für jede richtige Lösung erhältst du einen Punkt.

Meine Punkte: ☐ von 8

3 Speaking: Can you say it in English?

1 Please come to my birthday party./Can you …?
2 What do you want to do on your birthday?
3 What is your favourite food?
4 Do you like party games?
5 I'm not interested in models.

Für jeden richtigen Satz erhältst du zwei Punkte. Manchmal gibt es mehrere Möglichkeiten. Frag deinen Lehrer oder deine Lehrerin, wenn du dir nicht sicher bist.

Meine Punkte: ☐ von 10

4 Writing: My birthday

My birthday is always in school time. It's on 5th March.
My parents, my grandma and my brother give me presents.
My grandma's present is usually the best present.
My mum always makes my favourite chocolate cake.
I invite my best friends from school for my birthday party.
We eat my birthday cake and listen to music.

Für jeden richtigen Satz erhältst du zwei Punkte. (Wenn du nicht sicher bist, wie viele Punkte du dir geben sollst, besprich dich mit einem Partner/einer Partnerin.)

Meine Punkte: ☐ von 12

5 Grammar: this, that, these, those

Those/those/them; this; this/these;
these/these/these; those

Für jede richtige Lösung erhältst du einen halben Punkt.

Meine Punkte: ☐ von 5

Auswertung:
40–47 Punkte: Wirklich gut, Kompliment! Überlege, ob du nun auch mal neue Lerntechniken ausprobieren möchtest.
31–46 Punkte: Du kannst schon viel auf Englisch ausdrücken, musst dich mit manchem aber nochmal auseinander setzen. Sieh dir deine Fehler an – was genau hast du falsch gemacht? Befasse dich dann mit den Tipps.
30 Punkte und weniger: Du hast einiges aufzuholen. Nur keine Angst, das schaffst du! Nimm die Tipps unten ernst, und arbeite das *Theme* noch einmal durch. Vielleicht hilft dir ja ein Freund oder eine Freundin dabei.

Meine Punkte insgesamt: ☐ von 47

Lerntipps:
- **Listening:** Bei Höraufgaben wie diesen geht es nicht darum, dass du jedes einzelne Wort verstehst. Konzentriere dich vielmehr nur auf das, was gefragt ist, in diesem Fall die Daten.
- **Reading:** Wenn du einen neuen Text vor dir hast, ist es sinnvoll, ihn erst einmal nur zu überfliegen, damit du weißt, worum es geht. Lies ihn dann konzentriert, und zwar sooft du willst. Mache dir keinen Stress, wenn andere schneller sind als du. Es kommt zunächst erst einmal nur darauf an, dass du alle wichtigen Details verstehst.
- **Speaking:** Lies nochmal alle Texte im *Theme* durch, so kannst du dir Redewendungen gut merken.
- **Writing:** Falls du merkst, dass du beim freien Schreiben immer wieder dieselben Fehler machst, lege eine Fehlerstatistik in zwei Spalten an. In die linke schreibst du mit einem korrekten Beispiel die Art des Fehlers. Das, was dir Schwierigkeiten bereitet, markierst du (z. B. My mum makes a cake.). In der rechten Spalte führst du eine Strichliste. Wenn du so deine häufigsten Fehler ermittelt hast, kannst du leichter gezielt üben, um sie zu vermeiden.
- **Grammar:** Solltest du feststellen, dass es dir nicht immer ausreicht, den *LiF*-Teil zu lesen, um dir Regeln zu merken, dann lege dir zusätzlich ein spezielles Grammatikheft an mit allen Regeln, die dir Probleme bereiten. Überlege dir auch Beispielsätze. So kannst du gut kontrollieren, ob du die Grammatik tatsächlich verstanden hast. Falls du merkst, dass du bestimmte Regeln nicht verstehst, frage deinen Lehrer/deine Lehrerin um Rat.

Test yourself – Lösungen

Jetzt hast du schon ein ganzes Jahr mit *Test yourself* gearbeitet, weißt also, wie es geht: Vergleiche deine Antworten mit den folgenden Lösungen und zähle deine Punkte zusammen. Lies dann die Auswertung und die Lerntipps für die Sommerferien und nächstes Jahr, wenn es mit **Camden Market** weitergeht.

1 Listening: In a clothes shop

1 right   3 wrong   5 wrong   7 wrong
2 right   4 wrong   6 right   8 right

Für jede richtige Lösung erhältst du zwei Punkte.

Meine Punkte: von 16

2 Grammar: Present progressive

picture 1: *are sitting; are waiting*
picture 2: *is stopping; is flying; are watching*
picture 3: *are leaving; are jumping; is running*
picture 4: *are crossing; are laughing; are shouting*

Für jede richtige Verbform erhältst du einen halben Punkt.

Meine Punkte: von 5,5

3 Reading: Cybercamp

1–c)   4–b)
2–b)   5–b)
3–b)   6–c)

Für jede richtige Zuordnung erhältst du zwei Punkte.

Meine Punkte: von 12

4 Writing: A postcard home

Mögliche Lösung:
Hi Mum,
Everything is fine at cybercamp. I'm having a great time. It's cool. The teachers show us how to write computer programs. That's in the morning. In the afternoon, we do other things. We go swimming, play basketball or go to interesting places around Boston. The evenings are fun, too. We just talk and play computer games. The other children here are very clever. There's one boy from New York, Ken, he comes here every summer. Mum, can I go again next summer? Please!!! See you soon.
Love, Jimmy

Für jeden Satz, den du geschrieben hast, erhältst du zwei Punkte. (Wenn du dir nicht sicher bist, wie viele Punkte du dir geben sollst, besprich dich mit einem Partner/einer Partnerin.)

Meine Punkte: von 16

Auswertung:

41–49,5 Punkte: Prima, du bist auf dem richtigen Weg. Überlege trotzdem mal, welche Lerntechniken dir helfen, auch die wenigen Fehler, die du machst, zu vermeiden.
32–40 Punkte: Du hast schon viel gelernt, musst aber hier und da noch etwas aufarbeiten. Was sind die Knackpunkte? Lies die Tipps und befasse dich nochmal mit dem *Theme*.
31 Punkte und weniger: Das genügt nicht. Sei nicht zerknirscht deswegen. Du kannst ja noch aufholen. Die Tipps unten helfen dir. In den Ferien hast du viel Zeit, dich noch einmal intensiv mit dem Textbook und Workbook von **Camden Market** zu beschäftigen.

Meine Punkte insgesamt: von 49,5

Lerntipps:

- **Listening:** Nutze die Ferien, um häufig englische Texte auf Kassetten, CDs und im Fernsehen anzuhören. Versuche doch auch mal, einige Zeilen oder zumindest Wörter aus deinem derzeitigen Lieblingslied aufzuschreiben. Findest du heraus, worum es darin geht?
- **Grammar:** Du hast in diesem Lernjahr viele wichtige Grammatikregeln kennen gelernt. Hast du sie dir gemerkt? Wenn nicht, wiederhole gezielt Aufgaben zu denen, die dir entfallen sind. Und teste einmal, ob du frei über die Regeln sprechen kannst, also ohne in den *LiF*-Teil zu schauen. Dazu brauchst du nicht unbedingt eine zweite Person – sprich einfach mit dir selbst. Und denk dir zu jeder Regel einen Beispielsatz aus. So kannst du gut kontrollieren, ob du die Grammatik wirklich verstanden hast.
- **Reading:** Nimm dir in den Ferien fünf Texte aus dem Textbook vor, die dir Spaß gemacht haben, und fünf, die du besonders schwierig fandest. Arbeite sie gewissenhaft durch und sprich sie auf Kassette.
- **Writing:** Leg nicht gleich los, wenn du einen Text schreiben willst, sondern mache dir zuerst in Ruhe Notizen. Überprüfe dann, ob du deine Gedanken in einer sinnvollen Reihenfolge notiert hast. Falls nicht, nummeriere die einzelnen Stichworte. Anschließend kannst du anfangen zu schreiben.

Bildquellen:

4	Renate Krause, Ettlingen
19	Gabi Uplawski, Hannover (Camden Lock Uhr); Kirstin Jebautzke, Braunschweig (15 Uhr); age fotostock/Mauritius, Hamburg (7:26, 6:33 und 16 Uhr)
25	Nicole Bergemann, Berlin; Valerie Callaghan, Braunschweig (CSfG)
37	Gabi Uplawski, Hannover; Carol Pearson, Hannover (Primrose Hill Park)
51	RSPCA Photolibrary, Horsham (Tiger)
55	Andreas Schmidt, Hannover
73	Picturefile, David Graham
74	Sportimage/Action Images, Hamburg (Arsenal); Quick-Klick, Bad Vilbel

Diese Arbeitsanweisungen findest du in Camden Market:

Hier findest du eine Liste der Arbeitsanweisungen, die in deinem Workbook und im Textbook am häufigsten vorkommen. Du kannst hier immer dann nachschauen, wenn du sicher gehen willst, dass du eine Anweisung richtig verstanden hast.

Add …	Ergänze mit …
Answer the questions.	Beantworte die Fragen.
Ask questions and give answers.	Stelle Fragen und gib Antworten.
Check the order of …	Überprüfe die Reihenfolge von …
Choose the correct words/sentences/ … from the box.	Wähle das richtige Wort/den richtig Satz/ aus dem Kasten.
Circle the odd one out.	Kreise das Wort ein, das nicht zu den anderen passt.
Collect information/pictures/about …	Sammle Informationen/Bilder über …
Complete the sentences/sentence parts/ speech bubbles/the table …	Vervollständige die Sätze/Satzhälften/den Text/ die Sprechblasen/die Tabelle …
Correct the text.	Berichtige den Text.
Cross out the wrong …	Streiche die falsche … durch.
Describe the picture/photo/…	Beschreibe das Bild/Foto/…
Do the exercises.	Löse die Aufgaben.
Draw lines/a picture.	Zeichne Linien/Male ein Bild
Fill in the right words/the grid.	Setze das passende Wort ein/Fülle das Raster aus.
Find the right word/more words.	Finde das passende Wort/mehr Wörter.
Finish the report.	Schreibe den Bericht zu Ende.
Listen to the text/dialogue and …	Höre dir den Text/das Dialog an und …
Look at the picture/photo/the example/…	Sieh dir das Bild/Foto/Beispiel/… an.
Make a list …	Fertige eine Liste an.
Make a mindmap about food/free time/…	Lege ein Wortnetz zu Essen/Freizeit/… an.
Make notes.	Mache dir Notizen.
Match the sentences/sentence parts with the pictures.	Verbinde die Sätze/Satzhälften mit den Bildern.
Match the sentence parts.	Verbinde die Satzteile.
Number …	Nummeriere …
Put the words/pictures in the right order.	Bringe die Wörter/Bilder in die richtige Reihenfolge.
Read the text first.	Lese dir zuerst den Text durch.
Say it in English.	Sag es auf Englisch.
Tick (✓) the right words/sentences/pictures/answers.	Hake die richtigen Wörter/Sätze/Bilder/ Antworten ab.
Underline …	Unterstreiche …
Use these words/sentences/…	Benutze diese Wörter/Sätze/…
What is the solution?	Wie lautet die Lösung?
Work with a partner.	Arbeite mit einem Partner.
Write down the words/the past forms.	Schreibe die Wörter/die Vergangenheitsform/ … auf.
Write … sentences about your …	Schreibe … Sätze über deine …
Write the numbers in the boxes.	Schreibe die Nummer in die Kästchen.

Camden Market 1
Portfolio-Fragebögen

Name: _____

Klasse: _____

Liebe Schülerin, lieber Schüler,

vor dir liegt ein Heft mit Portfolio-Fragebögen.

Bei **Das bringe ich mit** kannst du eintragen, was du bereits im Fremdsprachenunterricht in den Klassen 3 und 4 gelernt hast.

Die anderen Fragebögen füllst du jedes Mal aus, wenn ihr ein *Theme* im Textbook und Workbook komplett abgeschlossen habt.

Das geht so:
Sieh dir z. B. den Kasten **Hören** an.
Lies die Sätze und überlege, wie gut du das kannst, was dort beschrieben ist.

Hinter jedem Satz steht, wo du nachschlagen kannst, wenn du nicht genau weißt, was gemeint ist.

Es kann auch sein, dass ihr im Unterricht nicht alle Übungen gemacht habt. Dann kannst du den betreffenden Satz überspringen.

Vor jedem Satz stehen zwei Punkte.

Wenn du meinst, dass du etwas schon gut kannst, dann male den <u>ersten Kreis</u> grün aus. 🟢 ⚪

Du bist dir noch nicht ganz sicher?
Dann male den <u>ersten Kreis</u> gelb aus. 🟡 ⚪

Lies dann auf der angegebenen Seite im Textbook oder Workbook nach und mache die Übung noch einmal.
Kannst du es nach der Wiederholung nun richtig gut?
Dann male den <u>zweiten Kreis</u> grün aus. 🟡 🟢

Wenn du weißt, dass du noch große Schwierigkeiten hast, dann male den <u>ersten Kreis</u> rot aus. 🔴 ⚪

Sieh dir die entsprechenden Seiten
im Textbook oder Workbook noch einmal gründlich an
und wiederhole die Übungen.

Kannst du es nun besser? Dann male den <u>zweiten Kreis</u> gelb aus. 🔴 🟡

Wenn du es nach dem Üben richtig gut kannst, dann male den <u>zweiten Kreis</u> grün aus. 🔴 🟢

Auf der letzten Seite findest du einen Fragebogen, in den du am Ende der Klasse 5 eintragen kannst, was dir am meisten beim Englischlernen geholfen hat.

Das bringe ich mit

Das bin ich

Ich heiße: _____

Meine Schule heißt: _____

_____

Bis jetzt habe ich ☐ 🇬🇧 ☐ 🇫🇷 gelernt.

Wie ich den Unterricht in der Fremdsprache bisher fand:

☐ Ich hatte viel Spaß, weil _____

☐ Ich hatte nicht so viel Spaß, weil _____

☐ Ich hatte überhaupt keinen Spaß, weil _____

Das habe ich schon gelernt:

Ich kann …

☐ verstehen, was mein Lehrer/meine Lehrerin sagt.

☐ eine Geschichte verstehen, wenn sie mit Bildern erzählt wird.

☐ eine Geschichte verstehen, wenn sie ohne Bilder erzählt wird.

☐ verstehen, wenn ich etwas gefragt werde, und darauf antworten.

☐ andere begrüßen.

☐ etwas über mich sagen.

☐ ein paar Lieder singen.

☐ ein paar Reime oder Gedichte aufsagen.

☐ englische oder französische Wörter lesen und verstehen.

☐ ein Bildwörterbuch benutzen.

☐ etwas abschreiben, ohne Fehler zu machen.

☐ _____

Das bringe ich mit

Ich kenne Wörter zu diesen Themen: viele ✓✓✓ einige ✓✓ wenige ✓

☐☐☐ Zahlen	☐☐☐ Spielzeug
☐☐☐ Farben	☐☐☐ Geburtstag
☐☐☐ Wetter	☐☐☐ Ostern
☐☐☐ Tiere	☐☐☐ Halloween
☐☐☐ Schulsachen	☐☐☐ Weihnachten
☐☐☐ Essen und Trinken	☐☐☐ Jahreszeiten
☐☐☐ Körper	☐☐☐ Wochentage
☐☐☐ Kleidung	☐☐☐ Monate
☐☐☐ Familie	☐☐☐ Ferien
☐☐☐ Zuhause	☐☐☐ Länder
☐☐☐ Hobbys	☐☐☐ London

Das sind meine Lieblingswörter in der Fremdsprache:

_____

_____

_____

Das gefällt mir besonders (✓) beim Sprachenlernen:

☐ Lieder singen

☐ Reime und Gedichte aufsagen

☐ Geschichten hören

☐ spielen

☐ kleine Stücke und Rollenspiele vorführen

☐ etwas lesen oder vorlesen

☐ etwas schreiben

☐ _____

Außerdem kenne ich folgende Sprachen:

_____

_____

Darauf freue ich mich im Englischunterricht in Klasse 5:

_____

_____

 # Was ich nach *Theme 1* schon kann

Hören

○ ○ Ich kann verstehen, was mein Lehrer/meine Lehrerin im Unterricht zu uns sagt. (TB S. 229)

○ ○ Ich kann anhand von Geräuschen und Wörtern heraushören, wo Personen sind. (TB A2)

○ ○ Ich kann eine Personenbeschreibung verstehen und weiß, zu wem sie passt. (TB B4c)

Sprechen

○ ○ Ich kann Dinge in einem Bild benennen. (TB A1, A3, B2, C1)

○ ○ Ich kann sagen, was ich habe, und fragen, was andere haben. (TB A3, C1)

○ ○ Ich kann mich und andere kurz vorstellen. (TB A5, A6, A7)

○ ○ Ich kann mich und andere beschreiben. (TB A7, B4, C4)

○ ○ Ich kann sagen, was ich mag und was meine Hobbys sind. (TB A10, C1, C4)

Lesen

○ ○ Ich kann die Aufgaben im Textbook und Workbook lesen und verstehen.

○ ○ Ich kann einen Comic verfolgen. (TB B1)

○ ○ Ich kann Texte gut verstehen, wenn ich mir die Bilder dazu genau ansehe. (TB A4, A9, B4, C2)

Das muss ich noch üben.

Das geht schon ganz gut.

Kein Problem!

Schreiben

○ ○ Ich kann Wörter fehlerfrei abschreiben. (WB 4, TB A4)

○ ○ Ich kann aus einem Text herausschreiben, was jemand hat oder sammelt. (TB C2, C3)

○ ○ Ich kann mit Hilfe einer Vorlage einen Text über meine Hobbys schreiben. (TB C4)

Lern- und Arbeitstechniken

○ ○ Ich kann mit einem Partner/einer Partnerin arbeiten. (TB A5, A7, B2)

○ ○ Ich kann in meinem Buch nachschlagen, um Informationen zu finden zu
 • Grammatikregeln (TB *LiF* ab S. 145)
 • den Wörtern aus *Theme 1* (TB *Words* ab S. 161)
 • Wortfeldern aus *Theme 1* (TB *Wordbanks* ab S. 138)
 • Tipps und Hilfen (TB *Toolbox* ab S. 129)

Wortschatz

○ ○ Ich kann ein Bild beschriften. (TB B2)

○ ○ Ich kann Wörter zu Wortfeldern zusammenstellen, z. B. zum Thema Körper oder Kleidung. (TB S. 138)

Was ich nach *Theme 2* schon kann

Hören

○ ○ Ich kann ein Lied verstehen, z.B. *Another Monday*. (TB A3)
○ ○ Ich kann einem Hörtext Bilder zuordnen. (TB A1c)
○ ○ Ich kann mir Notizen zu einem Hörtext machen. (TB C5)

Das muss ich noch üben.

Das geht schon ganz gut.

Kein Problem!

Lesen

○ ○ Ich kann eine Geschichte mit Bildern verstehen. (TB B4, B5)
○ ○ Ich kann Informationen aus einer Tabelle ablesen. (TB B9)
○ ○ Ich kann Texte so gut verstehen, dass ich Richtig- und Falschaussagen erkenne. (TB B7)

Sprechen

○ ○ Ich kann sagen, wie spät es ist. (TB B2)
○ ○ Ich kann meinen Tagesablauf beschreiben. (TB B3)
○ ○ Ich kann Wörter buchstabieren. (TB B10)
○ ○ Ich mich mit einem Partner/einer Partnerin über das Thema Schule unterhalten. (TB C4)
○ ○ Ich kann begründen, warum ich etwas mag oder nicht mag. (TB C9)

Schreiben

○ ○ Ich kann mein Traum-Klassenzimmer beschreiben. (TB A4)
○ ○ Ich kann einen Text verbessern. (TB B10)
○ ○ Ich kann mit Hilfe von Stichwörtern über Schulfächer schreiben. (TB C2, C4)
○ ○ Ich kann meinen Schulalltag beschreiben. (TB C6)

Wortschatz

○ ○ Ich kann mit Hilfe von Bildern neue Wörter lernen. (TB A1, A2)
○ ○ Ich kann Wörter in Wortnetzen zusammenstellen. (TB C3)

Lern- und Arbeitstechniken

○ ○ Ich kann mich auf einen neuen Text vorbereiten, indem ich Ideen sammle, worum es gehen könnte. (TB B4)
○ ○ Ich kann in einer Gruppe an einem Projekt arbeiten. (TB C4)

 # Was ich nach *Theme 3* schon kann

Hören

○ ○ Ich kann einen Songtext mithilfe von Bildern verstehen. (TB B4)
○ ○ Ich kann an Geräuschen erkennen, wo sich eine Person befindet. (TB C2)
○ ○ Ich kann Wegbeschreibungen auf einer Straßenkarte folgen. (TB C4)
○ ○ Ich kann hören, ob jemand eine *long form* oder *short form* benutzt. (TB C10)

Sprechen

○ ○ Ich kann beschreiben, wo sich Dinge in einem Raum befinden. (TB A1, A2)
○ ○ Ich kann jemanden fragen, wie sein/ihr Zimmer aussieht. (TB A2, A3)
○ ○ Ich kann eine Bildergeschichte nacherzählen. (TB B1)
○ ○ Ich kann meine Meinung zu einem Thema äußern. (TB B5)
○ ○ Ich kann Wegbeschreibungen geben. (TB C5)

Lesen

○ ○ Ich kann Texte über verschiedene Räume verstehen. (TB A2, A3)
○ ○ Ich kann sagen, welche Personen in einer Geschichte vorkommen. (TB B1)
○ ○ Ich kann Texten die passenden Bilder zuordnen. (TB C1)
○ ○ Ich kann Falschaussagen zu einem Text korrigieren. (TB C8)

Das muss ich noch üben.

Das geht schon ganz gut.

Kein Problem!

Schreiben

○ ○ Ich kann mit Hilfe von Fragen mein Zimmer genau beschreiben. (TB A4)
○ ○ Ich kann meine Aufgaben im Haushalt beschreiben.
○ ○ Ich kann eine Quizkarte anfertigen.

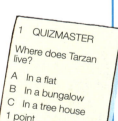

Lern- und Arbeitstechniken

○ ○ Ich kann mir eine Vokabelkartei anlegen. (TB S. 131)

Wortschatz

○ ○ Ich kann Wortfelder zum Thema Räume und Häuser anfertigen. (TB S. 131)
○ ○ Ich kann Gegensätze finden. (TB S. 63/2)

Was ich nach *Theme 4* schon kann

Hören

○ ○ Ich kann Fragen und Antworten in einem Hörtext zuordnen. (TB A3)

○ ○ Ich kann einen Hörtext verstehen, wenn ich mir vorher Gedanken zu dem dazugehörigen Bild mache. (TB B4)

Das muss ich noch üben.

Das geht schon ganz gut.

Kein Problem!

Lesen

○ ○ Ich kann eine Tierbeschreibung verstehen und weiß, welches Tier gemeint ist. (TB A1)

○ ○ Ich kann Informationen aus einem Text in einer Tabelle festhalten. (TB A1)

○ ○ Ich kann einen Comic lesen. (TB B1)

○ ○ Ich kann eine Broschüre lesen. (TB B9)

○ ○ Ich kann eine längere Geschichte lesen und den einzelnen Abschnitten Überschriften zuordnen. (TB C3)

Sprechen

○ ○ Ich kann Fragen über vergangene Ereignisse stellen. (TB A3, A6)

○ ○ Ich kann eine Geschichte mit Hilfe von Bildern und Stichwörtern erzählen. (TB B5, B8)

Schreiben

○ ○ Ich kann mein Lieblingstier beschreiben. (TB A1)

○ ○ Ich kann eine Geschichte mit Hilfe von Stichwörtern schreiben. (TB B8)

Wortschatz

○ ○ Ich kann Wortfelder zu verschiedenen Begriffen zusammenstellen, z. B. zu *wild animals, farm animals* und *pets*. (TB S. 143)

○ ○ Ich kann Gegensätze finden. (TB S.85/2, S. 189)

Lern- und Arbeitstechniken

○ ○ Ich kann eine Grammatikregel selbst herausfinden. (TB A2, S. 137)

○ ○ Ich kann Wörter im Wörterbuch nachschlagen. (TB B3)

○ ○ Ich kann die Bedeutung von neuen Wörtern mit Hilfe von Umschreibungen erschließen. (TB C3)

Was ich nach *Theme 5* schon kann

Hören

○ ○ Ich kann ein Lied mitsingen. (TB A2)
○ ○ Ich kann ein Telefongespräch über ein Geburtstagsfest verstehen. (TB B3)

Lesen

○ ○ Ich kann die Reihenfolge von Ereignissen in einer Geschichte festhalten. (TB A6a)
○ ○ Ich kann Falschaussagen zu einem Text korrigieren. (TB A6b)
○ ○ Ich kann eine Geschichte verstehen, nachdem ich die dazugehörigen Bildern beschrieben habe. (TB B1)

Sprechen

○ ○ Ich kann mit einem Partner/einer Partnerin einen Dialog nachsprechen. (TB A1b)
○ ○ Ich kann ein Einkaufsgespräch führen. (TB A3)
○ ○ Ich kann beschreiben, was gerade passiert oder was auf Fotos zu sehen ist. (TB A5, A6, B1, B6)
○ ○ Ich kann Vermutungen äußern. (TB B1)
○ ○ Ich kann sagen, was ich gerade tue. (TB B4)

Das muss ich noch üben.
Das geht schon ganz gut.
Kein Problem!

Schreiben

○ ○ Ich kann ein Einkaufsgespräch schreiben. (TB A1d)
○ ○ Ich kann Bilder beschreiben. (TB B2)
○ ○ Ich kann begründen, warum mir ein bestimmter Monat gut gefällt. (TB B10)
○ ○ Ich kann erzählen, was ich an meinem Geburtstag mache. (TB B11)

Wortschatz

○ ○ Ich kann Wörter zu einem Oberbegriff zusammenstellen. (TB A2c)
○ ○ Ich kann Wortkarten anfertigen, die mir helfen, ein Gespräch zu führen. (TB A3b)

Lern- und Arbeitstechniken

○ ○ Ich kann eine Grammatikregel erkennen, wenn ich Beispiele aus Texten sammle und vergleiche. (TB B5)
○ ○ Ich kann mit einem Partner/einer Partnerin arbeiten. (TB B6)
○ ○ Ich kann in einer Gruppe an einem Projekt arbeiten. (TB A3, C-Teil)

Was ich nach *Theme 6* schon kann

Das muss ich noch üben.

Das geht schon ganz gut.

Kein Problem!

Hören

○ ○ Ich kann aus einem Sportreport heraushören, wer welche Sportart macht. (TB A1b)

○ ○ Ich kann verstehen, welche Informationsquellen verschiedene Sprecher nutzen. (TB B1b)

Lesen

○ ○ Ich kann Fragen zu einem Text beantworten. (TB A2, C1c)

○ ○ Ich kann Bilder einem Text zu ordnen. (TB A5, B1)

○ ○ Ich kann Falschaussagen zu Texten korrigieren. (TB A8, C1b)

Sprechen

○ ○ Ich kann verschiedene Sportarten benennen. (TB A1)

○ ○ Ich kann ein Interview führen. (TB A1d, B6)

○ ○ Ich kann sagen, wo ich Informationen finde. (TB B1)

○ ○ Ich kann mit einem Partner/einer Partnerin ein Verkaufsgespräch führen. (TB B3)

○ ○ Ich kann mit einem Partner/einer Partnerin über Freizeitaktivitäten sprechen. (TB C2)

Schreiben

○ ○ Ich kann über meine Lieblingssportarten schreiben. (TB A10)

○ ○ Ich kann eine E-Mail schreiben. (TB B5)

○ ○ Ich kann eine Postkarte schreiben. (TB C5)

Lern- und Arbeitstechniken

○ ○ Ich kann eine Geschichte verstehen, wenn ich vorher Stichworte zum Thema sammle. (TB A6)

○ ○ Ich kann die W-Fragen zu einem Text beantworten. (TB A7, S. 132)

○ ○ Ich kann Informationen in einer Tabelle festhalten. (TB C1a, C4b)

Wortschatz

○ ○ Ich kann Wörter zu verschiedenen Themen gruppieren. (TB A4)

○ ○ Ich kann in 30 Sekunden ____ (Anzahl) Wörter zu einem Thema sammeln. (TB A9)

○ ○ Ich kann englische Worterklärungen verstehen. (TB B4)

Was mir in Klasse 5 beim Englischlernen geholfen (✓) hat:

Hören
Hörtexte verstehe ich am besten, wenn ich
- ☐ vorher schon eine Idee habe, worum es gehen könnte.
- ☐ den Text mitlesen kann.
- ☐ mir beim Hören Notizen mache.
- ☐ dazu Bilder sehe.
- ☐ _____

Sprechen
Sprechen fällt mir leicht, wenn ich
- ☐ einen Dialog mit einem Partner/einer Partnerin führe.
- ☐ mir vorher Notizen mache.
- ☐ etwas auswendig lerne, z. B. Reime.
- ☐ viel über ein Thema gelesen habe.
- ☐ _____

Schreiben
Schreiben gelingt mir am besten, wenn ich
- ☐ mich an eine Vorlage oder einen Mustertext halte.
- ☐ mir erst einmal Notizen mache.
- ☐ meinen Text durchsehen und bearbeiten kann.
- ☐ _____

Lesen
Lesetexte verstehe ich am besten, wenn ich
- ☐ mir vor dem Lesen Bilder und Überschriften ansehe.
- ☐ mir vorher überlegt habe, was wahrscheinlich im Text vorkommen wird.
- ☐ den Text mit einem Partner/einer Partnerin besprechen kann.
- ☐ meine Gedanken zu dem Text auf einen Zettel schreibe.
- ☐ _____

Wortschatz
Wörter lerne ich am besten, wenn ich
- ☐ etwas dazu aufmale.
- ☐ sie oft laut spreche.
- ☐ sie in einem Wortnetz oder Wortfeld aufschreibe.
- ☐ sie häufig wiederhole.
- ☐ _____

Grammatik
Grammatik verstehe ich am besten, wenn
- ☐ mir jemand die Regeln erklärt.
- ☐ ich die Regeln selbst herausfinde und aufschreibe.
- ☐ _____

Das habe ich in diesem Jahr besonders gern gemacht: 🙂

_____

_____

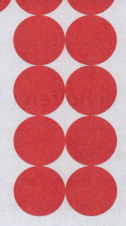

www.diesterweg.de